JOHN BOYANA RADASI

Missionary to Zimbabwe

Jean Nicolson

FREE PRESBYTERIAN PUBLICATIONS

Free Presbyterian Publications
133 Woodlands Road
Glasgow
G3 6LE

ISBN 0 902506 38 2

Printed by
Pioneer Press Limited
Skipton
North Yorkshire

Contents

Rev John Boyana Radasi.

CHAPTER ONE

Family Background

IN the 1890s preparations were made throughout the British Empire to celebrate Queen Victoria's Diamond Jubilee on 22 June 1897. After reigning for 60 years the Queen was now well-known throughout Europe and the British Empire. Her reputation as "the Great White Queen" had reached even remote parts of Africa, so that David Livingstone, the Scottish missionary-explorer, was once asked, "How many cows does the great Queen have?"

In the Transkei, a small part of Britain's Cape Colony in South Africa, a choir was formed to join in these Jubilee celebrations in the United States of America. One of the members of the choir was a young man called John Boyana Radasi. He was later to become the first missionary of the Free Presbyterian Church of Scotland in what was once called Southern Rhodesia but is now known as Zimbabwe. This came about in a remarkable way.

No one knows exactly when John Radasi was born, but it was probably sometime during 1876. He was brought up in a Christian home in Seymour, Transkei. His father was a godly man and a preacher, who also worked for the Government. He was a court interpreter, but he also had a contract to carry letters and parcels between his home village and Readesdale, some miles away. He owned 40 acres of land and was obviously a man of ability and enterprise.

The Radasi family belonged to the Fingo tribe which had settled about 1824 on the banks of the Kei River, on the eastern borders of the Cape. Some years before that, the Fingoes and many smaller tribes had fled southwards down the east coast of South Africa from Zululand, where they had been terrorized by the Zulu chief, Chaka, who was known as the African Napoleon.

In many ways the Fingoes were a remarkable people. One of the missionaries who worked among them gave this testimony: "They had been decimated by many years of inter-tribal warfare, by oppression, and even by slavery, but had emerged by 1873 as a highly intelligent, hard-working people, skilled in agriculture and with a great thirst for education." This desire for education was stimulated by their contact with students who had trained at Lovedale Institution, Cape Colony, a school which taught both practical and academic subjects to African men and women. Only a few of the Fingoes were Christian at this time.

In 1873 the Fingo headmen sent a message to Rev James Stewart of Lovedale. It was expressed in their own picturesque way: "We desire to have a school, a child of Lovedale, a shadow-of-rest for our children." Although Dr Stewart was deeply involved in his work as Principal of Lovedale, he made a three-day journey in a horse-drawn vehicle to Fingoland over a rough, and sometimes dangerous, road. When he arrived he found a great gathering of Fingo men and women waiting for him. Several orators from the crowd, both men and women, spoke eloquently of their hopes for a school in their own area.

Dr Stewart suggested that they collect £1,000 among themselves and he promised to collect another £1,000 from business men in the Cape and from friends in Scotland. The Fingoes collected £1,450, far more than had been suggested to them. Each man gave five shillings (25 pence today, but at that time it would buy far more than it does now), and when Dr Stewart arrived to collect the money one of the headmen said,

6

A kraal in Zimbabwe.

"Here are the stones. Now build!" Building work began in 1875, when Dr Stewart brought with him four masons from Aberdeen, Scotland, and £1,500 in fulfilment of his promise. The building eventually cost £7,000, and the Fingoes continued to pay for it until the debt was cleared.

The school was named Blythswood after Captain Blyth, the Fingoes' magistrate, who encouraged them in every worthwhile scheme. The fact that every man began by giving five shillings towards the cost of the school, and continued to give until the debt was paid off, was something entirely new among the tribes. As Dr Stewart's biographer wrote, "The liberality of the Fingoes was as definite a discovery as gold on the Rand and diamonds at Kimberley". By 1880, after years of faithful missionary work among them, half of the Fingo people claimed to be Christian. It was from this enterprising people that the Radasi family came.

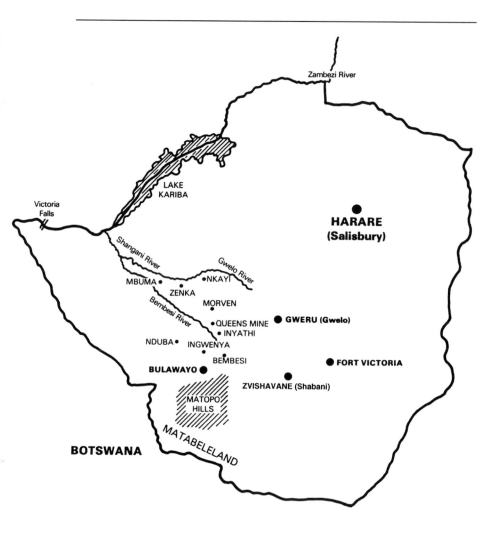

Zambezi River

LAKE KARIBA

Victoria Falls

Shangani River

HARARE (Salisbury)

Gwelo River

MBUMA

NKAYI

ZENKA

MORVEN

Bembesi River

QUEENS MINE

GWERU (Gwelo)

INYATHI

NDUBA

INGWENYA

BEMBESI

FORT VICTORIA

BULAWAYO

ZVISHAVANE (Shabani)

MATOPO HILLS

BOTSWANA

MATABELELAND

ZIMBABWE

As Lovedale will often appear in our story, we may look for a little at how this mission station started. It lies near the eastern border of Cape Colony, and was founded by the Glasgow Missionary Society in the 1820s, when there was still very little interest in missionary work in the Church of Scotland.

In 1841 the Rev William Govan, a fine missionary and a gifted teacher, became head of the Mission. In his first school he had eleven African and eight European pupils. The European children were the sons of missionaries, magistrates, or traders, who until then had no school within their reach. One of the African boys arrived at the school clad only in a sheepskin, but he so far outshone the other pupils that some years later he graduated from Glasgow University. He was the first translator of *The Pilgrim's Progress* into si-Xhosa, the Fingo language, and earned the respect of Africans and Europeans alike as a minister of the gospel in Cape Colony.

Mr Govan retired in 1870, and Dr Stewart became Principal in his place. The Free Church of Scotland supported the Mission and the name Lovedale was chosen in honour of the respected Glasgow minister, Rev John Love, who took a great interest in mission work. The Lovedale staff at that time all came from Scotland. Dr Stewart brought out workmen from Aberdeen to set up industrial training for men, as well as making provision for teaching the more usual school subjects. Similarly, women were given a thorough training in what were then called domestic subjects.

Someone said of Dr Stewart: "He was a sincere Christian and all he did was governed by his desire to conform to the spirit of the gospel. His aim was to uplift the African by touching him at every point of civilized life and fitting him for all Christian duties." A worthwhile work indeed!

• CHAPTER TWO •
Scotland

NOTHING is known of John Radasi's boyhood, nor of the school he attended in Seymour, but it was obvious in later years that he had a good general education, and that he spoke excellent English.

Probably before he was 20 years old he left for the United States as a member of his choir. It was while he was there, it would seem, that John Radasi was converted. It would be very interesting to know how he was brought to a knowledge of the Saviour, but there seems to be no record available.

While he was in the United States, John Radasi made friends with another young African, James Saki. They heard that Scotland was a very religious country where there were good preachers, so they decided to go to Scotland on their way home to South Africa. Having crossed the Atlantic they sailed from London to Leith, and paid for their passage by working as members of the crew of the ship. After landing in Leith they made their way to the neighbouring city of Edinburgh.

John Radasi and James Saki duly arrived in Edinburgh, and after finding somewhere to stay, they found their way to Lothian Road. There they stopped on the edge of the pavement, feeling rather lonely and sad. In the Lord's providence they stood opposite the house of a Free Presbyterian lady, Mrs

Sinclair. Her son looked out of the window and saw the two African men and was immediately interested; he had lived in South Africa for some years and had learned one of the African languages. He went outside to speak to them.

After greeting them and asking them where they had come from, he invited the two men into his mother's house. Mrs Sinclair welcomed them and quickly prepared tea. Mr Radasi asked God's blessing on the food, and soon they were engaged in an interesting conversation which indicated that Mr Radasi was a spiritually minded man. Mrs Sinclair knew that the Rev Neil Cameron, then a Free Presbyterian minister in Glasgow, was prayerfully interested in beginning foreign mission work. She sent him a telegram which read, "I have your missionary". Mr Cameron replied, "Send him along".

At this time the Free Presbyterian Church of Scotland was only three years old. In 1892 the General Assembly of the Free Church of Scotland had passed by a huge majority what they called a Declaratory Act. Those who opposed the Act rightly saw it as an attack on the doctrines of the Westminster Confession of Faith, and on the Bible, on which these doctrines were based. When, in 1893, the Free Church refused to repeal the Act, two ministers, some students for the ministry, many elders and thousands of other men and women left the Free Church to form the Free Presbyterian Church of Scotland.

These were difficult times. There were very few ministers. There were few churches or manses. There was very little money available, but there was a warm interest in foreign mission work, and many were praying that the Church would get an opportunity to send out its own missionary to a foreign field.

Mr Cameron was greatly attracted to Mr Radasi, especially to his obvious piety and his gentle, unassuming ways. The two Africans were introduced to members of the Church's Synod, and it was decided to open a Foreign Mission Fund. Both men were received by the Church as students for the ministry, Mr Radasi in 1896. In 1900 Mr Saki left the Free Presbyterian Church and joined the Plymouth Brethren, whose views he now shared.

Mr Radasi made it known that he had a great desire to go as a missionary to Matabeleland in Southern Rhodesia (now Zimbabwe). He knew that some of his own Fingo people had gone there from the Transkei at the invitation of Cecil Rhodes, well-known as an Empire builder and at one time Prime Minister of Cape Colony, South Africa. He knew also that the language of the Matabele people was somewhat similar to that of the Fingoes. Although the gospel had been preached in parts of Matabeleland before Mr Radasi went there, he wished to work in an area where no one had yet gone with the gospel.

A few years earlier Matabeleland had been the scene of fierce fighting between the pioneer settlers and the Matabele. In 1893 the king, Lobengula, fled and the British Chartered Company took control. Rhodes was very interested in the occupation of Matabeleland; he was very astute and believed that the Fingoes of the Transkei were friendly to the British. So he felt that it would be helpful to his plans if some of them went to live in Matabeleland. A number of the Fingoes who accepted Rhodes' invitation were fine Christian men.

Mr Radasi's course of study in preparation for his work as a missionary included some time spent in Edinburgh at Heriot Watt College (now a university) and at the Free Church's teacher training college. He later studied Systematic Theology, Church History and some Hebrew and Greek under the Church's tutors, Rev J R Mackay in Inverness and Rev Donald Beaton in Wick.

In 1904 the Synod appointed a Foreign Mission Committee; the members of the Committee were the Rev J S Sinclair, Convener; the Rev Neil Cameron and the Rev J R Mackay. The Committee was to make arrangements for Mr Radasi to begin mission work in Matabeleland.

By 1904, his eighth year in Scotland, Mr Radasi's studies were drawing to a close. He was a fluent English speaker, and had proved himself to be an able preacher. He quickly became familiar with the Biblical form of worship in his new Church, including the use of nothing except the Psalms in metre for

Part of the Radasi family:
Malixan (a daughter-in-law), Mrs Julia Radasi, Mabel and Mildred (daughters).

praise in public worship. In the Highland congregations he noted with interest the custom of "putting out the line" (the precentor singing each line of the Psalm on his own before the congregation sang it together). In later years on the mission field he made use of this form of singing because there were so few Psalm books.

When the Synod met in November 1904, Mr Radasi had completed his studies. They received a report that his examinations were satisfactory and decided that his ordination should take place at a meeting of the Southern Presbytery on the next evening, 16 November 1904. At this service Rev John Macleod of Kames in Argyllshire preached the sermon. His text was from the Gospel of John 8:36, "If the Son therefore shall make you free, ye shall be free indeed". The official record states: "The Moderator after special prayer did in the name of the Presbytery, and by the authority of the Divine

Head of the Church, ordain and set apart to the office of the holy ministry as a missionary of the Church the Rev J B Radasi." Later in the service the Moderator gave him suitable advice about his duties and work.

Everybody felt sorry for the young missionary going away alone. Rev Neil Cameron summed up their feelings: "The fact of Mr Radasi having to go alone caused us all to feel sad. It dawned on the minds of some how sympathetic the Lord Jesus was to the frailty of human nature when he sent out his disciples by twos."

To make it easier for Mr Radasi to begin his work in Matabeleland, the Church got in touch with some people of influence who could help him by giving him letters of introduction or recommendation. Among them was the Member of Parliament for Inverness, Sir R B Finlay, who wrote to the Colonial Secretary, a Government minister in London. The Colonial Secretary made arrangements with the officials of the Chartered Company in Salisbury (now Harare) in Southern Rhodesia, so that they would give Mr Radasi all the help they could in carrying out his work. This proved very useful to Mr Radasi.

The Church's Foreign Mission Committee also got in touch with the Bible Societies to find out if there were metrical Psalms in the language of Matabeleland. There was no success at first, but the Clerk of the Committee said that he would continue to make enquiries.

• CHAPTER THREE •
From Scotland to Africa

BY December 1904 Mr Radasi was ready to set off for Africa to begin his life's work in what was then called Southern Rhodesia. Mr Angus Fraser went with him on the first part of his journey and saw him to his ship at Southampton. Mr Fraser was an uncle of Rev J S Fraser, who many years later became a successful missionary in Southern Rhodesia, until his death in 1959, aged only 45.

While in London Mr Radasi and Mr Fraser called on the Colonial Secretary, the British Government minister responsible for other countries ruled by Britain. He received them very kindly and sent a letter on Mr Radasi's behalf to Lord Milner, who was at that time Governor of the Cape Colony. The Colonial Secretary told them that they should also see the Secretary of the Chartered Company which at that time controlled Southern Rhodesia. They took his advice, and after their visit the Company's Secretary sent a copy of Mr Radasi's certificate of licence and ordination to their office in Cape Town.

After parting with Mr Fraser at Southampton Docks Mr Radasi went aboard his ship. A quiet voyage brought him to Cape Town, where he spent a few days with a married sister. He called on the local secretary of the Chartered Company, who asked him many questions about himself and his family. At last he asked Mr Radasi if he had a letter of introduction to Rev Neville Jones, who was a member of the London Missionary Society in Bulawayo, Southern Rhodesia, and a minister of the United Free Church. When Mr Radasi said he did not have such a letter, the Secretary said he could do nothing to help him. It must have been a great disappointment, especially when the Company's official in London had been so helpful. Mr Radasi said afterwards that he believed the Secretary in Cape Town had taken him for a member of the Ethiopian Church, which the Chartered Company was trying to suppress in Cape Colony and Natal.

Mr Radasi then went to see the General Manager of the railway company, and he was very helpful. He advised Mr Radasi as a minister of the gospel to travel second class: he could then travel at half price and he would get the use of a bed on the train. The journey would take three days and his fare would cost £4 11s. 6d. (£4.57 in today's money). Mr Radasi left by train for Bulawayo on Thursday the 16th of December and stopped for the Sabbath in Mafeking, a town in Bechuanaland, now Botswana. On the afternoon of the next Tuesday he arrived quite alone in Bulawayo; he was a complete stranger.

Southern Rhodesia was completely different in its political order from Cape Colony, where Mr Radasi had grown up. The Government at the Cape had been largely influenced by missionaries who had come out to South Africa inspired by the spirit of the eighteenth-century Evangelical Awakening in England. Many of the repressive laws were no longer in force.

Let us now sketch briefly the background of the people among whom Mr Radasi had come to work. The Matabele had their origin in Zululand in eastern South Africa; their founder and leader was Mzilikazi, son of Matjobana. To escape from the stronger armies of Chaka, the Zulu chief, Mzilikazi and his people fled westwards from Zululand about the year 1820. They crossed the Drakensberg mountains into the Transvaal, destroying and conquering the Sotho tribes during the following 15 years, but absorbing their women and children into the now increasing Matabele nation.

The Matabele were only one section of the Bantu tribes of South Africa on the move as a result of the aggression of Chaka, and as the other tribes were set in motion there was a trail of destruction resulting from those inter-tribal wars. After some years on the move Mzilikazi with his people settled at Moseka in the Marico Valley in the Northern Transvaal. Mzilikazi was a brilliant soldier and the Matabele nation was highly organized and disciplined. They had learned to use the military methods introduced by Chaka: the pincer movement of attack to encircle the enemy, and the use of the short, stabbing spear in close combat, with the defensive ox-hide shield.

However, another group of people on the móve had also entered these parts. It was the time of the Great Trek northwards by the Voortrekker Boers, Dutch farmers from Cape Colony who were armed with guns. There was conflict between the two groups, and after their defeat by the Boer leader, H Potgieter, at Moseka in 1837, the Matabele moved onwards north of the Limpopo River to the grassy plains beyond. "We are going to the country of the Mambo," Mzilikazi had declared. (Mambo was the famous king of the tribes across the Limpopo River.)

It was not difficult for them to conquer the people of those grassy plains, for in 1831 there had been an earlier invasion of Bantu from the south led by Zwangendaba, also fleeing from Chaka of Zululand. They sacked the religious and government centre, Great Zimbabwe (Zimbabwe means the graves of the Chiefs), and destroyed the kingdom of the Rozwi which was the ruling family of those parts. The Mambo (king), Charisamuru, had moved near Inyathi and was cruelly put to death by them, before they proceeded north of the Zambezi River. Now the Matabele came and took control of the area, absorbing the native Makalanga people into their nation. Mzilikazi himself had his settlement near Ntabazika Mambo,

from the King's army were posted to watch for their return, and when Moffat arrived at the King's kraal he was greeted with a fearsome display of thousands of armed Matabele in battle array. However, when this ceremony was over, Mzilikazi gave Moffat a warm welcome and was soon won over by Moffat's manly, fearless and disarming friendliness. Mzilikazi developed such a deep-rooted affection for the missionary that he addressed him as Baba (father). As a token of his regard, the King and his headman Mncumbata travelled with Moffat on his wagon for part of the way back to Kuruman.

In 1840 Mzilikazi heard that Moffat was in Natal and sent an envoy under the guidance of a European hunter to search for Moffat. However, Moffat was already on his way to see his old friend. Mzilikazi was suffering from dropsy and Moffat was able to treat the King successfully. Moffat had set out with goods for his son-in-law, David Livingstone, who was exploring in the region of the Zambesi River, and the goods eventually reached Livingstone through the good offices of the King.

The next time Moffat visited Mzilikazi, in 1857, the missionary went specially on behalf of the London Missionary Society to ask for permission to begin work among the Matabele. At first Mzilikazi did all he could to discourage Moffat, but he eventually agreed — if Moffat himself would come. Moffat agreed to send his son instead; he himself was growing old, and he still had work to do at Kuruman.

On 26 December 1859, after a journey of many months from Cape Town by ox-wagon, Robert Moffat led a band of missionaries including his own son, John Smith Moffat, to Matabeleland to begin mission work. They were kept waiting anxiously for several weeks beside the Bembesi River before Mzilikazi gave a definite promise that they could start a mission. Robert Moffat wrote, "Satan is making a desperate effort to shut the doors against the blessed gospel".

Eventually they were allowed to settle in a valley near Inyathi. There they suffered incredible hardships for over 20 years without a single convert, but when advised to close

Another kraal.

down the work their reply was: "The sword can blot out the Matabele, the gospel alone can save them. The Committee are of the opinion that the present staff should be increased." However, in later years they had many fine Christians both at Inyathi and at Hope Fountain, a second station opened near Bulawayo, as a result of patient missionary work and the blessing of God. One of their converts, Makhazo Mkala, was put to death later on, because he was "a follower of the Book", so becoming the first Ndebele martyr.

After spending several months helping the missionary party to settle in, Robert Moffat bade a final farewell to his friend Mzilikazi who, sadly, never became a Christian. Harold Child, who was a Rhodesian Under Secretary of Internal Affairs, writes in his history of the Matabele: "This great friendship between a heathen potentate and a Christian missionary was the most extraordinary ever to be recorded in South African history."

On the right is Ma Hlabangana, who had been one of
King Lobengula's chief wives.
After a visit to Durban she said: "The wonderful sea, it stretched so far
before me, yet it was always coming towards me.
It was like the mercy of God."

Hartley, who was believed to have shot over 1,000 elephants. These hunters became friends of Mzilikazi and the young Lobengula, who went with them on hunting expeditions. The most outstanding of the hunters during Lobengula's reign was Selous, who later, in 1890, acted as guide to the Pioneer Column, the first white force which invaded the area; they went on to Mashonaland, bypassing Bulawayo, Lobengula's capital.

From the middle of the nineteenth century, after people had the chance to read the books he had written about his travels, David Livingstone's explorations in central Africa became widely known. It was a time when many people in Britain and in other parts of Europe began to take an interest in this part of the world. This was the era of "the Scramble for Africa", when many of the nations of Europe, in their rush to build up their own empires, scrambled to bring as much of Africa as possible under their own control.

their new rulers and because of the way the black police were abusing their power. There were several disasters in the country too: a severe drought, a plague of locusts and thousands of cattle dying of a disease known as the rinderpest. Then, only three years after the end of the previous war, the country was again torn asunder by strife between black and white, when the Mashona and the Matabele rose against the British.

In this dangerous situation David Carnegie, a missionary who belonged to the London Missionary Society and was stationed at Hope Fountain, went at great risk to himself into the Matopos area, near Bulawayo. This was a place sacred to the tribes, and there Carnegie made contact with an induna (headman) called Hoti, who controlled 800-1000 men. After two days of difficult negotiations he persuaded Hoti to meet Rhodes the next day. Mzilikazi's only surviving widow, Nyambezana, helped in these negotiations between Rhodes and the African chiefs in the Matopos hills. Rhodes never forgot the actions of this old woman, and it is a well-known episode in Matabele history.

At a meeting in the Matopos hills Rhodes earned the admiration of the Matabele by appearing unarmed with a few friends before a thousand armed Matabele. Rhodes seated himself on a large boulder and insisted that before negotiations could begin the warriors must lay down their arms. This they did. Then Hoti set out all their grievances. He gave an assurance that he would not again try to rebel and accepted Rhodes' promise that all injustices on the other side would be removed. Peace was made without signing any documents; each side trusted the other to keep to the terms of the agreement.

Carnegie, the missionary, continued to feed the starving Matabele people at Hope Fountain Mission during the difficult months ahead. The London Missionary Society recorded: "Carnegie and Selous, the famous South African hunter, made an appeal to the authorities that evil-doers only should be punished, and not all Africans indiscriminately."

Southern Rhodesia had now been for 12 years under the government of the British Chartered Company when Mr Radasi arrived in Bulawayo. The Matabele were under severe restrictions and were not allowed to move around the country, or even within the town, without a pass, a kind of identity card which allowed the police to check the movements of migrant workers on farms and in mines; but the main reason for the pass was to prevent another surprise attack on the whites.

only £300. He saw the comfortable manses built for the ministers of the various denominations, but when he wrote to Rev J R Mackay in Scotland he identified himself with the Church there: "I know that we do not have the means to build churches and manses nor to pay evangelists, for we are a poor, struggling church, but I often think of what you said, 'The salvation of one soul is to God worth more than the whole material universe'."

Mr Radasi found the laws in Matabeleland very different from the laws in Cape Colony. He now required a pass to go from one town to another, and another pass to visit in the evenings. There was practically no means of transport, so it was difficult to travel about the country. Horses died when they were bitten by the tsetse fly. Only well-off Europeans and the police had horses; the missionaries used bicycles. The country was still thickly forested, with grass at times six feet high, and crossed by footpaths except where a road led to a European farm. The railway had only recently been extended northwards through Gweru and on to Salisbury (Harare). White farmers used mules for ploughing as they were not affected by the bite of the tsetse fly, but the Africans had to make do with primitive ploughs and hand tools when they tilled the soil.

Mr Radasi began preaching wherever he could find an opening. In Bulawayo the Matabele lived in small two-roomed brick huts in locations of their own, while the white population lived in small towns or on their farms or at their mines. Of course Bulawayo was much smaller then than now; it had a population of around 6,500. Lions and leopards, elephants and wild dogs roamed the countryside, and there were many crocodiles in the larger rivers.

The surrounding country was divided into large farms of three or four thousand acres, most of them in the possession of white farmers or owned by the Government. A few of the larger missions had farms of three thousand acres because they wished to keep some of the good land for the Matabele. Many of the Matabele lived on the farms as tenants and paid a small rent, but when the land changed hands the new owner might move the Matabele off the farm whether they had anywhere to go or not. Only a few farmers allowed the Africans to build churches or schools on their land.

After the take-over by the Chartered Company most of Matabeleland was opened up to white settlement. But two large areas along the Gwaai and Shangani Rivers were set aside for the Matabele only. These were the first Reserves created in Rhodesia. These forest areas were not developed and were less fertile than the central plateau, where the white farmers had land. In a letter to a friend in Scotland Mr Radasi refers to the Sabbath-breaking in Bulawayo among the Europeans, where horse-racing, gambling and sports were all pursued on the Lord's Day. He had a love for the Sabbath and he was saddened by the sin he was seeing around him.

CHAPTER EIGHT

New Friends

YOU will remember the young Fingo porter who listened to Mr Radasi's conversation with Rev J Mfazi at Bulawayo railway station. When, the next weekend, young Stephen Hlazo went home to Bembesi, about 30 miles north of Bulawayo, he told his father what he had heard at the station. His father, John Hlazo, was an educated man and a sincere Christian; he knew Cecil Rhodes personally and had been a driver for a time on the Zeederberg mail van, which travelled between Kimberley and Bulawayo before the railway line was laid.

John Hlazo was at once interested when he heard that a Presbyterian minister had come from Scotland. So he and a few of his friends went to Bulawayo to look for Mr Radasi, but they had to wait for a few days till Mr Radasi returned from a preaching trip. He had gone 90 miles farther south to a place called Gwanda using a donkey-cart and a few donkeys which Mr Mfazi had lent him. When Mr Radasi arrived in Gwanda, a small settlement where a Government official was stationed, he went among the people inviting them to attend a service at a pre-arranged spot. The people were discouraged by the drought which had distressed the country for some months, and their reply to Mr Radasi was, "Yes, we shall gladly come

A pole and daga church at Zenka.

to hear you if your God will give us rain". No doubt with a silent prayer, Mr Radasi replied, "Yes, come".

When the people gathered for the service Mr Radasi noticed a large black snake emerge from the bushes. He was afraid the people would scatter and he set about to kill it, which he did. It is possible that the people looked on the snake as a promise of rain. However that may be, they listened attentively to Mr Radasi as he preached. Towards evening a black cloud appeared on the horizon, followed by a heavy downpour of rain to the great joy and relief of all. No doubt this answer to prayer encouraged the new missionary.

When Mr Radasi got back to Bulawayo he found the Fingo men waiting for him, and one can imagine how he rejoiced to find that at least some of them were Christians. After discussion his new friends told him that he could settle among them if they were able to get the consent of an Ndebele chief of high rank, who lived not far from Bembesi. He was Chief Ngege, who had been born a chief in the days of Lobengula. Mr Radasi, always resourceful, hired four donkeys, and a wagonette with accommodation for sleeping, and set off with his new friends for Chief Ngege's home.

The Chief received them kindly and offered Mr Radasi ten acres of land on which to build a church, a school, and a home for himself. He also said that he would like his own children to go to the school. The Chief chose a site on an elevated piece of ground between two rivers. Mr Radasi would also have to get permission from the District Commissioner, a Government official. He proved to be very helpful and friendly and gave him permission to go ahead. No doubt Mr Radasi showed him his letters of recommendation from the Colonial Secretary in London. The District Commissioner told Mr Radasi that he could have a lease of the site at £1 per year, and that the lease could be renewed each year. The site of the new mission was called Ingwenya (crocodile) after one of the rivers flowing nearby.

Before parting with Mr Radasi, Chief Ngege produced a pile of letters. The Chief was not able to read, but his son had been writing him over a period of six months from South Africa, where he was possibly working in one of the gold mines. When Mr Radasi read out the names of his relatives from the letters, the Chief asked in great surprise: "How do you know their names when you have never met them?"

John Hlazo offered Mr Radasi a room in his house at Bembesi until he had a home of his own. He also gave a large room where he could hold services. When he wrote to Scotland, Mr Radasi said, "I have a great responsibility as a missionary among the heathen, and need the prayers of the Lord's people that I may get grace and strength to discharge faithfully all the duties I may be called upon to perform". He then quoted the words of Psalm 2: "Ask of Me and I shall give Thee the heathen for Thine inheritance, and the uttermost parts of the earth for Thy possession." He went on: "I am glad to inform you that the Administrator in Salisbury (a

Government official) has greatly interested himself in our Mission, and has instructed the Company representative in Bulawayo to assist me in every way. I applied for a Certificate of Exemption (from carrying passes) which was immediately granted."

Mr Radasi had decided to live out in the country and not in town. He told the Rev Neil Cameron: "It is absolutely necessary for me to have a church before the rainy season sets in in November. A thatched square building of pole and daga (mud) will cost about £35. Doors and windows must come from Bulawayo. An African man from Cape Colony will build it for me." He also mentioned in his letter how grateful he was to the Mfazis for their kindness to him since his arrival in Bulawayo. His boxes and other luggage were still in their manse, but, as he explained in his letter, it would be necessary for him to move from Bembesi and live among the people at Ingwenya.

The Committee in Scotland suggested to Mr Radasi that he should have a wooden house built for himself. A Scotsman in Bulawayo offered to build such a house in Bulawayo and to transport it and assemble it again at Ingwenya for £81. The Church people in Scotland gave generously for the work — one friend giving £41. (Remember that this could buy very much more then than it does now.) Mr Radasi's salary amounted to £80 per year, but when the Church in Scotland realized the high cost of living in Rhodesia it was increased to £100. The Church sent out £35 for the building of the church, £81 for Mr Radasi's house and what was needed for doors and windows, which were to come from Bulawayo. With the help of the people in Scotland Mr Radasi bought a small Cape cart and four donkeys so that he could get around more easily to take services in the surrounding district.

For three months the local men had been digging for water on the Mission site. They had dug about sixty feet but had not been successful in finding water. The soil, however, was becoming damp, and they had come across a few frogs. It was taken as a hopeful sign.

• CHAPTER NINE •
Becoming Established at Ingwenya

DURING 1905 only a few of the Matabele attended church. They were poor and were scantily clothed, and some of them made this an excuse for staying away. None of them could read or write, so Mr Radasi began to teach them to sing by reading the line, as he called it — reading out each line of the Psalm before the congregation sang it. You may remember that he was a trained singer, and he took great pains to teach them to sing correctly.

Apart from preaching the gospel, Mr Radasi's great aim was to teach the people to read, so that they would be able to read the Bible for themselves. He was also very anxious to obtain the Psalms in metre in the si-Xhosa language, or in Zulu. To his delight Mr Radasi found that there were nine Zulu Psalms in the Wesleyan hymn-book and some time later his Fingo friends pointed out that there were many portions of the si-Xhosa Psalms in the Presbyterian hymn-book. Mr Radasi used this selection over the years. He wrote to Dr Stewart of Lovedale to ask if it would be possible to have the whole book of Psalms put into si-Xhosa metre. Dr Stewart sent back a favourable reply, but shortly afterwards he took ill and died. So at this time nothing came of the request.

Before the end of 1905 Mr Radasi opened a school but few children came, and those who came attended very irregularly. In fact, the parents did not want their children to go; they believed that the children would be more useful to them herding the cattle and so they thought they should be paid for attending school. Mr Radasi began a night-school for young men who worked during the day; this was very successful and over the years a number of the young men were converted. Time and again Mr Radasi asked his friends in the Church in Scotland to pray that "Ethiopia would soon stretch out her hands to God".

Mr Radasi kept up a regular correspondence with these friends in Scotland. He wrote to Mr Cameron: "The poor Africans are full of superstition; they believe very much in witchcraft. Anybody who is ill is thought to have been bewitched, but they dare not put anyone to death under British rule. Before the ploughing season comes, an African (witch) doctor is called to come with some medicine to doctor the seed."

Mr Radasi remarked in one letter that polygamy (the practice of men having more than one wife) and superstition seemed to be a great hindrance to the gospel. Mr Cameron replied that God's truth would prevail and that Satan could neither resist its power nor keep it from bringing forth fruit in some. Mr Radasi's reply was, "O for the grace of faith to believe that truth".

About this time Mr Radasi referred to the death of his uncle, who was a lay preacher in the Transkei: "My uncle is dead. He died a little over two months ago, and his last words were, 'I am going home. I am going to rest for ever, but I cannot help but weep when I think of the mercy of the Lord to such a great sinner as I am.'"

During 1905 there was a great drought in the country. Rain had not fallen for ten months. The smaller rivers had dried up, and the people had to walk six miles to the nearest large rivers, which were often infested with crocodiles. The Matabele became very restive; they consulted their witch-doctors but, of

Mealies for distributing during a famine.

course, that did no good. A number of their chiefs went to Bulawayo to demand that the large statue of Cecil Rhodes be removed from its place on Main Street because, they said, it prevented the rain from coming. The local magistrate tried to pacify them; he assured them that the statue had nothing to do with the drought. The chiefs argued that the previous year, when the statue had been erected, very little rain had fallen, and none at all since then. They threatened to send their men to remove it.

Chief Ngege was not among those chiefs. Instead, he sent a message asking Mr Radasi to hold a prayer-meeting. He had heard that, when some other missionaries had prayed for rain, their prayers were answered. Mr Radasi agreed, saying that only God could send rain. The new church had been completed, but it had not been plastered for lack of water. However, that was of no immediate importance, and he announced a prayer-meeting. There was still no furniture in the church, but a table and two chairs were placed at one end; one chair for the minister and one for Chief Ngege.

There were 300 people at the meeting, including the Chief and 200 of his people. As they entered the building they saw a huge snake coiled in the centre of the floor. The people were delighted as they believed it was a sure sign of rain, but Mr Radasi insisted that it should be killed as its bite was very poisonous. There was some grumbling when this was done, but the service began.

Mr Radasi read the fourteenth chapter of Jeremiah slowly and distinctly. He had just read verse 7, "O Lord, though our iniquities testify against us, do Thou it for Thy name's sake; for our backslidings are many; we have sinned against Thee", when he was interrupted. To his surprise the Chief rose to his feet and, addressing the people, he said: "Say this after me, 'We have sinned against Thee'." Mr Radasi knew that it was a common occurrence in some churches for the people to stand up and speak or ask questions during the service. But he explained that no one should interrupt the service; anyone who wanted could ask questions afterwards.

That evening the rain came down in torrents, and it went on until the next day. The following week there was a second prayer-meeting to give thanks to God. This time the Chief did not attend; he had seven miles to walk from his home, and it had rained for several days. Travelling would now have been extremely difficult.

While this wonderful answer to prayer was most encouraging to Mr Radasi, there were other matters which discouraged him. He was specially sorry that there were still so few people coming to the services. On Sabbath mornings Mr Radasi held a prayer-meeting at 7 am. There were two preaching services, the first at 11 am and the second half an hour after the first finished. There was no evening service as night fell at 6.30 pm in winter and 7 pm in summer, and some people had to walk several miles to their homes. There was also a Bible Class for young men who had learned to read.

Chief Ngege had promised to send his son, Ndabana, to school but so far he had not done so. The people would follow the Chief's example, and if he sent his children to school they would send theirs. Mr Radasi promised a Bible in si-Xhosa to every child who learned to read the language. Every child who learned to read English would receive an English Bible. In one of his letters Rev Neil Cameron quoted Joshua 1:9, "Be strong and of a good courage; be not afraid, neither be thou dismayed; for the Lord thy God is with thee whithersoever thou goest". Mr Radasi found it very encouraging.

Mr Radasi wrote to Mr Cameron: "A friend in Scotland promised me some Bibles before I left. I would be very glad to have them as soon as possible. I would also like you to send me English Psalm books in metre. Of course, only a few can read yet, but I should like to have them in stock, also the Shorter Catechism. I am still anxious to get the si-Xhosa Psalms in metre and am hopeful that the Lord will open up a way. I have with me £3 given to me by some friends in Scotland for the translation and printing of the Psalms, and I am very thankful to them. If you have an old Confession of Faith, or two or three of them, I shall be glad to have them.

"The African people here are polygamists and Chief Ngege himself has four wives. None of his wives was present at the service for rain. Polygamy seems to be a great hindrance to missionary work. Please pray for me that the Lord might give me the spirit of prayer to keep me dependent on Himself."

• CHAPTER TEN •

Growth in the Church

THE year 1906 brought real encouragement. A Fingo Chief, Garner Sojini, joined the Church, the first Fingo to do so. A converted man, he had been attending services at Bembesi, ten miles from Ingwenya. Later, after moving to his new home at Selukwe, over 100 miles east of Ingwenya, he began to hold services.

There were also six Fingo men belonging to the Presbyterian Church of South Africa, and living at Bembesi, who asked to join the Free Presbyterian Church of Scotland. Mr Radasi went over the most important parts of the Westminster Confession of Faith with them and explained how the Free Presbyterian Church differed from other Presbyterian churches in doctrine, worship and practice, and also where they agreed. Then, after the men had taken time to consider what they were told, they returned to say that they accepted it all. Some of these men became preachers on the Mission, which was a great help to Mr Radasi as it left him free to go to other places to preach. And, thinking of the great gospel God had given him to preach, he asked in a letter to Scotland: "Is it not a great blessing to poor, hell-deserving sinners like ourselves that the invitations of the gospel are addressed to those who have destroyed themselves and a free pardon offered to guilty, lost sinners?"

About this time, in December 1906, Mr Radasi married a fine Christian girl, Annie Hlazo, a daughter of John Hlazo, who had already shown himself such a good friend to Mr Radasi and to the Mission. A Bulawayo minister performed the ceremony, but Mr Radasi himself took the opportunity to address all the people present, who included Chief Ngege. To have a Christian wife was a great support and comfort to Mr Radasi in his home, and in his preaching and teaching. About that time Mr Radasi asked the Foreign Mission Committee in Scotland for permission to visit his home in the Transkei, and that permission was readily granted.

It is very clear from Mr Radasi's letters to the Committee in Scotland how very careful he was in detailing exactly what it cost him to build the church, and to buy his own house and a Cape cart and donkeys. He regularly sent receipts for very small amounts and one cannot help feeling that his concern to be so exact was part of his gracious character. He also responded very graciously to any loving warnings or advice he received. On one occasion Mr Radasi wrote in reply to a letter from Mr Cameron: "You may be sure I was very glad to receive your words of exhortation. It is true what you say; there is great need that we continually exhort one another to hold firmly and faithfully to the Word of God, the Confession of Faith and to purity of worship, and we need to be reminded of our ordination vows. The days are evil, and we need special grace to enable us to hold fast the truth as it is in Christ Jesus."

The school which Mr Radasi had begun at Ingwenya was becoming better known. Two young brothers of the Makalanga tribe came 100 miles from the south of the country to be taught, so that when they went back they could teach their own people. Mr Radasi told them that they could stay if they built themselves a hut. This they did. They knew in any case that they would have to bring their own food, so they left home with two bags of mealie-meal, to cook porridge with, but one of the bags was lost or stolen on the train.

After some months at Ingwenya, Malatse Makalanga became very ill. Mr Radasi read the Bible to him and prayed

GABON

CONGO

ZAIRE

UGANDA

KENYA

RWANDA

BURUNDI

TANZANIA

ANGOLA

ZAMBIA

MALAWI

MOZAMBIQUE

Zambezi River

MASHONALAND

HARARE ●

ZIMBABWE

● Inyati

● Bulawayo

MATABELELAND

Beira ●

NAMIBIA

BOTSWANA

INDIAN
OCEAN

KALAHARI DESERT

TRANSVAAL

Limpopo River

ZULULAND

SWAZI
LAND

Kuruman ●

ORANGE FREE STATE

ATLANTIC
OCEAN

Orange River

NATAL

LESOTHO

TRANSKEI

CENTRAL
AND
SOUTHERN
AFRICA

SOUTH AFRICA

Blythswood ●

Lovedale ●

CAPE COLONY

East London

CAPE TOWN ●

with him each day, but Malatse used to cover his head with his blanket. He showed no interest in what Mr Radasi had to say; he was very superstitious and said that he had been bewitched by his people at home as they did not want him to come. Mr Radasi wrote to a friend: "He gave me great anxiety for his eternal welfare. However, towards the end, for he passed away, he began to listen with great interest when the Word of God was read, and before he was taken away gave every evidence, as far as I can judge, that he was a sinner saved by grace." It must have been a comfort to Mr Radasi to believe that there was at least one sinner now in heaven, who was blessed during his time in Ingwenya.

People near and far now began to show their confidence in Mr Radasi as a teacher. Chief Ratilani, a brother of Khama, the well-known Christian King of Bechuanaland (now Botswana), took his own son and the son of a headman all the way to Mr Radasi to be educated. The boys were Sechuana-speaking so they now had to learn Zulu. Two other young men came a distance of at least 200 miles from across the Zambezi River to be at his school. Several little orphan children were also brought to him to be cared for and taught. Mr and Mrs Radasi now also had a baby girl of their own, whom they named Mabel.

At last Chief Ngege sent his son Ndabana to school. He lived on the Mission and was allowed to go home on Fridays, but was told to return on Saturdays so that he could attend the Sabbath services. By now Mr Radasi was reporting that services were being held in two additional places. One was Bembesi, where the six Fingo men lived who had joined the Church, and the other was a place called Koco, six miles from Ingwenya where there was a small Matabele congregation. Mr Radasi wrote: "Our men at Koco have already cut poles and thatching grass in order to build a hut we can use as a church. One man, not belonging to our church, has lent his wagon and mules to carry the poles and grass to the proposed site."

In May 1908 Mr Radasi was able to tell the Committee in Scotland that he had baptized eight infants, children of believing parents, and also two adults who had not been

Murray Farm school.

baptized in their infancy: "They were well-reported of by our men and gave full satisfaction to the questions asked. Others also were examined who professed their faith in Christ and their obedience to Him, but gave no satisfaction to the questions asked, and so I had to defer their baptism. I usually defer baptism several months after they have given evidence of having been changed by the grace and Spirit of God in order that I may have good grounds to hope that God has wrought a work of grace in their hearts." Mr Radasi concluded his letter: "These are dark days, and we need special grace to keep us, and the Spirit of the Lord to guide us in everything we do. A divine work has been done for us, and what we need is that a divine work should be done in us by the Holy Spirit." By October 1909 Mr Radasi was able to say that the services were much better attended and that the people seemed anxious to hear the Word of God.

CHAPTER ELEVEN

A Visitor from Scotland

AS early as July 1907 Mr Radasi wrote asking for a visit from one of the Scottish ministers. He wanted the support, even for a short time, of one of his brother ministers, but he also wished that a minister of his own Church would baptise their daughter. So when the decision had been made he wrote: "It gave our people great pleasure to hear that a Committee has been appointed to arrange for a deputy to come out to Matabeleland."

In the same letter Mr Radasi acknowledges the receipt of Zulu Bibles and New Testaments. He had been checking the si-Xhosa translation of the Shorter Catechism with Scripture proofs which he had also been sent. "As far as I can see, it is a good and correct translation of the Shorter Catechism," he added.

In 1909 the Rev J R Mackay, came as a deputy from the Church in Scotland. He went by sea to Cape Town, and from there he made the long train journey of three days and nights to Bulawayo, where Mr Radasi met him and gave him a warm welcome. The two ministers took another train to Bembesi, 30 miles farther on, where they were met by a driver with a Cape cart drawn by four donkeys. They set off for Ingwenya, another ten miles over a rough road, crossing a bare, red-soiled countryside and passing through a ford across the Bembesi River and through several small dry river-beds — there had been no rain for six months and the weather was hot and the air dry. Here and there they could see occasional large trees, mostly thorn, and clusters of round huts known as kraals.

In writing home to Scotland Mr Mackay described that part of the country as being healthy and not too hot, 4,000 feet above sea-level — about the height of Ben Nevis, Scotland's highest mountain. "The Mission," he wrote, "is situated on a ridge of elevated ground which separates two rivers, and in almost every direction the view is open for many miles around. Although the situation is a very healthy one, Mr Radasi has been unable to get water on the site." At Ingwenya Mr Mackay found seven buildings, including the church. One of the buildings was covered with corrugated iron and consisted of a study and a bedroom, with a verandah in front. This was where Mr Mackay stayed while he was on the Mission. Round about there were large trees which gave a cool, welcome shade.

On Saturday the Mission reminded Mr Mackay of a pious Scottish home, as care was taken to have enough water drawn from the well and other preparations made so that no unnecessary work was done on the Lord's Day. About 6.30 am on Sabbath morning the bell rang for the prayer-meeting. The bell was actually nothing more than a large piece of metal dangling from a tree, which one of Mr Radasi's pupils struck with an iron tool.

About 100 people came to the first service, which began at 11 am. Sadly, Chief Ngege who had been very friendly to Mr Radasi and had given the first ten acres of land, became ill and died two weeks before Mr Mackay arrived. He had expressed pleasure in looking forward to him coming and he had hoped to be present at the first service.

Usually on Sabbath the second service was held an hour after the first, but Mr Mackay was afraid of the heat and the second service did not begin until 5 pm. Not so many people were there as usual because some of the congregation had several miles to walk to their homes. "It was my impression that I was helped in speaking to the people," wrote Mr Mackay, "and I believe that Mr Radasi is an excellent interpreter (into Sindebele). Chief Sojini had come the long way from Selukwe, and Mr Radasi's good friend and father-in-law, John Hlazo, was also there. The majority of the congregation consisted of Matabele, and they could easily be distinguished from the Fingoes, as the Matabele have a transverse slit in the lobe of their ears."

When he reached home after Mr Mackay's first service at Ingwenya Chief Sojini sent the following letter, which Mr Radasi translated into English:

"We are thankful to you for the visit you have paid us here in Africa, to come and pray for us. Oh, what great love you have shown our souls by crossing the waters of the ocean! May God keep you and make you return safely to Scotland, to tell them about Africa and its people, and what you have seen with your own eyes. We also thank the Church in Scotland for its sympathy for us, for having sent you here to Africa at great expense, through their love to us. They sympathise with us because we are blind. We see the power and love of Christ. With these words I send my greetings. I again thank the Church in Scotland. May you have a safe voyage home.

Yours truly,
Garner Sojini."

On the second of the five Sabbaths of Mr Mackay's visit, he and Mr Radasi went to Bembesi, ten miles from Ingwenya, in the little Cape cart. The church there had been gifted by the Chiefs, Sojini and Sibindi. Mr Radasi held a Sabbath school between the two services. They also went to Koco where they were given a hut to keep the service in. Mr Mackay enjoyed taking many of his services in Matabeleland, and not least the one with the few people who gathered to hear him at Koco. In further letters to Scotland Mr Mackay tells how, on his fifth

After a service in a classroom at Mbuma school.

Sabbath at Ingwenya, elders and deacons were ordained and some people were baptised.

The week before he left the Mission, Mr Mackay visited the village or kraal of the late Chief Ngege, which was on a European farm. He wrote: "It is a small circular enclosure consisting of a number of round huts where ten to twenty families live. I endeavoured to speak to them on John 3:16. The kraals or villages are not numerous in the Ingwenya area. Indeed, I do not know of any of considerable size with the exception of the late Chief Ngege's. As a rule one finds the Africans scattered over the country in single or double huts, and those at some distance from one another. Where the people are most numerous the land is most fertile and usually British farmers are in possession. The surrounding country was at one time thickly forested but the trees have been cut down to a large extent, and paths lead from one village to another."

In another letter Mr Mackay spoke about how "British farmers are to an increasing extent taking possession of the most fertile, and at the same time the most populous, parts of Southern Rhodesia, (which) has led almost all the denominations sending missionaries to the country to take steps to secure from the Government large farms in connection with the mission stations. This they do at once in order that the Matabele may not be dispossessed of all the best of the land, and also that their missionaries may visit and preach to the Matabele whose homes are on those farms."

Mr Mackay did not forget his fellow-countrymen from the Scottish Highlands who were living in Bulawayo. On his second visit to Bulawayo he preached a Gaelic sermon in the Presbyterian Church "to a fair gathering of Highlanders hailing from Sutherland, Ross, Inverness and Argyll, what is reckoned to have been the first Gaelic sermon ever preached in Rhodesia". To show their appreciation they presented him with a valuable gift. Then he recorded his departure: "I bade farewell to our dear friends at Ingwenya on the Tuesday after the second Sabbath of November. They, too, showed their gratitude for the Church's interest in them by presenting me with a valuable jackal-skin rug. I felt very much drawn to our people and parted with them with regret."

Mr Mackay noticed the high regard in which Mr Radasi was held by the white officials in Bulawayo, and the respect and affection his own people had for him. He summed up his thoughts: "My distinct impression is that it is a Mission which the Lord is blessing and will bless. Of course, the salient fact, the fact outweighing all other facts, whether favourable or unfavourable, is the desirable possession by the Mission of the constant goodwill of Him who said, 'I am the God of Abraham, the God of Isaac, and the God of Jacob. I have surely seen the affliction of My people and I am come down to deliver them.'" Mr Mackay went on to pay his own tribute to Mr Radasi: "He continues the same sensible, unwavering character which we always found him to be. A promising circumstance is the firmness with which purity of worship as well as soundness of doctrine is being upheld at the Mission. Mr Radasi has only a few Psalms in metre which he can use, but to these he adheres."

Perhaps the most important result of Mr Mackay's visit to the Mission was that he made arrangements for putting the si-Xhosa Psalms into metre. While he was in Rhodesia Mr Mackay wrote to Professor Henderson of Lovedale asking him to enlist the help of some of the Lovedale men in preparing a metrical version of the si-Xhosa Psalms, and in such metre as would allow them to be sung to Scottish Psalm tunes. Professor Henderson wrote back to say he had written about the matter to the Rev John Knox Bokwe, a missionary in South Africa, and a skilled linguist. Mr Bokwe agreed to undertake the work with the help of a Mr W K Ntsikana.

Mr Radasi was delighted to learn that the people at Lovedale had produced a new edition of the Shorter Catechism in si-Xhosa. It had been translated from English by the Rev John Bennie of Nechra, near Lovedale, and was highly prized by the Presbyterian ministers of those days. "It was very good of the Lovedale press to reprint it," Mr Radasi wrote to the Rev Neil Cameron; "I have given away a good number, not only to my scholars, but also to grown-up people and to people of other churches who have asked for them." Professor Henderson invited Mr Mackay to visit Lovedale on his way home to Scotland but this was not possible as he had already arranged to return home by the East Coast of Africa and then on through the Mediterranean.

Then, soon after Mr Mackay reached Scotland, this letter arrived from Mr Radasi: "I have received a letter from Lovedale to inform me that they have translated as far as the nineteenth Psalm. Do you not see now that your visit here was greatly blessed by the Lord? It has been the means of our getting the Psalms translated and put into metre.

"Last week I went to Selukwe with one of our elders. The school is now closed for a few weeks. We went to visit Chief Garner Sojini, who is one of our preachers, and to see the few families belonging to our Church there. I preached to them on the Sabbath. They were all very glad to see me. Chief Garner Sojini has been conducting services every Sabbath on behalf of our Church. He and his wife and family were the first Fingoes who joined our Church. He is living on a farm which he has rented from the agents. The farm belongs to Dr Sawer, a European gentleman who is at present living in London. Selukwe is a hundred miles from here. I presented Chief Sojini on behalf of our Church with one of the larger si-Xhosa Bibles, a pulpit Bible. He was an elder before he joined our Church. You will remember him visiting Ingwenya when he came to see you."

• CHAPTER TWELVE •

Witchcraft and Sabbath-Breaking

AT the end of January 1910 Mr Radasi was reporting what followed the death of Chief Ngege: "His death also caused a great commotion among his heathen people, who foolishly went to a witch-doctor to ascertain the cause of his death. The witch-doctor said that he had been bewitched and the persons who had bewitched him were Mleya and his wife. Mleya was Chief Ngege's brother, and the reason why he bewitched him was because he wanted to be chief in Ngege's place and also to secure his inheritance."

Mleya and his wife were therefore driven out of their kraal by the heathen people and had it not been for British rule they would have been killed on the spot. As Mleya and his wife were now living on a European farm the farmer brought a court action against the witch-doctor and his assistant. When the case went before the High Court of Bulawayo the judge sentenced the old witch-doctor to two and a half years in prison with hard labour, and his assistant to six months. The judge also said that he wished all Africans to know that no witchcraft — whether the powers came from on high or not — would be allowed, but would be suppressed with a firm hand.

Mr Radasi added: "I hope that the case will have a salutary effect on all witch-doctors. The heathen are steeped in superstition and believe very much in witchcraft. May the Lord in His mercy hasten the day when the Kingdom of darkness will be destroyed and the Kingdom of grace advanced, and when many may be brought to the knowledge of the truth as it is in Jesus Christ!"

At the same time Mr Radasi gave his thoughts about the visit of his friend from Scotland: "We were all very glad to have Mr Mackay with us. His visit has greatly strengthened the cause here, and I myself was encouraged and strengthened by it. Even the chiefs and people took a great interest in his visit here. One chief came 100 miles to see and hear Mr Mackay preach, and I also noticed many new faces which had never been to the services before, (people) living a long way from the Mission who are now regular attenders in our church. The women who were baptized by Mr Mackay, and the men also, are very regular in their attendance at the services, although they have five miles to walk in order to come to the services.

"It is a custom with some of the heathen Africans to make great beer-drinking parties and to kill a sheep or a goat and invite a large number of the people to come and assist them in weeding their lands. They do this by turns. I am sorry to say that even on the Sabbath Day this weeding of lands is being done by the heathen. But the Lord has shown His displeasure at that Sabbath-breaking in a very remarkable way. An uncivilized African named Xahana, living about a mile from our Mission here, invited a great number of heathen people, men and women, to come and assist him in weeding his lands on the Sabbath day. He had ordered a barrel of beer to be made. This attracted a large number of heathen and they all went with their hoes to the land. They were not long there when the clouds began to gather and it rained, and so they went home for a time.

"On their way home the lightning uprooted a large tree just in front of them, and threw it at them. They all fell down stunned, but none of them was killed, and so some of the

Dunga (seated) and Mildred Radasi (right) with a friend.

women returned home at once to their own homes, but the rest went to Xahana's house to wait there until the storm had passed over, so that they might go again to weed his land. The storm passed in a short time and they set out again to weed his lands. As soon as they arrived in the lands and before they started to work, the clouds gathered again and it began to rain, and the lightning uprooted another tree which was on the land they were about to weed. They were all so alarmed that they all returned to their homes without going to drink the barrel of beer that Xahana had made for them.

"His crops have now withered and he will not be able to reap anything from that land, whereas the crops belonging to the other Africans are still in good condition. Some of the women who were there and who came to the services the following Sabbath were saying that they will never again go and weed lands on the Sabbath day, and that what had happened that day had taught them a lesson which they will never forget. 'We now see that Mlimo (God) does not wish people to weed their lands on the Sabbath Day.'"

Mr Radasi was concerned for the physical health of his people as well as for their spiritual welfare. There was a great deal of malaria in the country, and in several letters he expresses his regret that he had no medical knowledge. "I would like you to send me a book on medicines like yours," he wrote to Mr Mackay; "all the missionaries have some knowledge of medicine, which is of great help."

CHAPTER THIRTEEN

The Death of Mrs Radasi

IN 1910 a great personal sorrow came to Mr Radasi. His young wife died after an illness of only 11 days, leaving behind not only a mourning husband but a two-year old daughter. It was with wonderful and gracious submission to his God that he wrote: "It is with deep sorrow that I have to inform you of the death of my wife after an illness which lasted about eleven days. She caught a cold in the lungs and everything that could be done was done for her, but it pleased the Lord to take her away from us. Her removal will cause a great blank in our church here." The people also were grieved over Mrs Radasi's death as she was a gentle, loving person. "She was truly a help-meet to me and was greatly devoted to our Cause here," Mr Radasi also wrote; "all our people here feel her loss very much."

He also recorded some more details of her last days: "Although she was so very ill and suffering great pain, the end came to us somewhat unexpectedly. The day that she died she seemed to be somewhat better. She was able to speak a little and to take a little food. One of the elders of our Church came to see her, and as we thought she was asleep we did not waken her. After he had gone she said, 'No, I was not asleep. It was strange for him to come and see me and go away again without praying.'

Some ladies from Zenka.

"At another time her mother wakened her to give her a little food, thinking she was asleep as her eyes were closed. She said, 'Mother, why did you waken me? I was not asleep but I had such a wonderful train of thought. You disturbed me by waking me up.' I used to watch the time to give her her medicine, which the doctor said was to be given three times a day. I had given it to her in the morning and at dinner-time, and while I was sitting beside her she called me nearer to her and said, 'I want no more medicine but prayer'. These were the last words she spoke to me, and at her request I prayed. She died the same night."

The Rev J R Mackay paid his own tribute: "I count it a privilege that I made the late Mrs Radasi's personal acquaintance, and I mourn with heart-felt sorrow on account of her early removal. She belonged to the Fingo people and was one of the gentlest of creatures. What was much more, she appeared to be a true child of God. Mr Radasi spoke to me, I think more than once, of the great comfort he enjoyed in respect that Mrs Radasi was so thoroughly in sympathy with his views of doctrine and worship."

Three years later in 1913, Mr Radasi lost both his father and eldest sister in the Transkei. His father had been converted under the preaching of the early missionaries, but he became unhappy about new and unscriptural practices which later missionaries had brought into the church. He was very ill for 14 days, and as he was no longer able to read for himself, he asked that the Word of God should be read to him. Shortly before he died he asked that the eighth chapter of Romans be read, and when the eighteenth verse was read he asked that the verse be repeated: "For I reckon that the sufferings of the present time are not worthy to be compared with the glory which shall be revealed in us."

Mr Radasi went to visit his now widowed mother. He then travelled to Lovedale to see what progress was being made with the Psalms but to his disappointment he found that they had not yet started to print them.

• CHAPTER FOURTEEN •

A New Church
at Ingwenya

DURING 1913 Mr Radasi was able to report that the
congregation at Ingwenya had increased. The school roll was
also bigger; 70 children were now attending. Mr Radasi
himself taught in the school for four days in the week, as well
as taking an evening class for young men who were working
during the day.

In fact so much progress had been made at Ingwenya, under
the Lord's blessing, that a new and larger church was required.
The new church was built in 1913 by a Bulawayo builder. It
was arranged that the bricks should be made locally to save
expense. The whole cost was to be £400. Collections were
made among the people for seats. Some people gave sheep,
goats or maize instead of money, and the Church then got
money by selling the animals. The seats cost £24 and were all
paid for in this way. The Church in Scotland sent out the
balance of £232 required by the builder in Bulawayo.

About this time both a day-school and a night-school were
opened at Morven, some 12 miles from Ingwenya. Several
heathen families there began to attend the church services
regularly. Services were also begun at Florida Mine, a gold

Mrs Julia Radasi.

mine a few miles from Ingwenya. Unlike other mines no work was done there on the Lord's Day. The manager of the mine gave a large hut where services could be held, and he also wished a school to be opened for the children of the men who worked there.

There was a heathen kraal near the mine where the headman was known as Sibindwana. His son and daughter began to attend the services and were converted. His wife also used to attend occasionally, but Sibindwana himself never went to the services. Several young men at the mine professed faith in Christ and were baptised. Mr Radasi wrote to Scotland: "We need the prayers of the Lord's people that the kingdom of grace (might) be advanced and the kingdom of Satan destroyed."

The hut at Florida Mine where services were held was destroyed by dynamite, but the manager rebuilt it at his own expense. When Mr Radasi spoke about what happened he added, "It is wonderful to see the kindness of the Lord, that He should make the mine manager take an interest in our work".

Mr Radasi had continued with the Bible Class and he wrote to Rev Neil Cameron: "I am pleased to say that nearly all the members of my Bible Class have professed conversion and have been baptised. A good number of those in the Bible Class have learned to repeat the Shorter Catechism answers. We have a notorious witch-doctor attending church just now. His name is Ingelwano. One of our elders, Patrick Mzamo, a man powerful in prayer, and a greatly exercised Christian, preaches at Koco, a few miles from Ingwenya, every Sabbath." (He was the father of Rev Petros Mzamo, who still ministers at Mbuma, about 100 miles from Ingwenya.)

In 1915, Mr Radasi, a widower now for five years, married a daughter of Chief Garner Sojini of Selukwe. Over the years they had four sons, Malixan, Dunga, Langa, Edwin, and a daughter, Mildred. You may remember that the daughter of the first marriage was Mabel. She married in due course and left the district. Dunga was sent to South Africa to live with a clergyman relative of Mr Radasi's, and to be educated there. Edwin was taken to Scotland by the Rev John Tallach in 1932. After his return to Ingwenya he eventually set up an independent church. The youngest daughter, Mildred, also married and left Ingwenya district.

Mr Radasi was greatly cheered by the conversion of the late Chief Ngege's son, Sigogo. In a letter to Mr Cameron he writes: "You will, I believe, be glad to hear of the conversion of Chief Ngege's eldest son, who took his father's place. He is Ndabana's eldest brother. He formerly had three wives but since his conversion he sent two of his wives back to their homes, and he now has only one wife, who has also been converted, and they both attend the services here very regularly every Sabbath although they live some distance away — I think probably three or four miles away. They are living on a farm. The farmer is opposed to missions and he does not want anyone to hold services on his farm, but does not object to people on his farm going to any church service elsewhere."

Sigogo himself told about how he first became concerned about his soul: "I never used to pray at all. I hated going to church, and hated missionaries as well, as you yourself know that I very seldom attended a place of worship, and I did not even want my wives to go to church. But one night, as I was in my hut, a thought came to me that if what the minister had said is true then surely I am lost, and if I were to die now I would go to hell. I tried to put that thought away from me, not to think of these things at all, but it would come back to me.

"I then began to pray secretly, and used to go out even in the night to pray. And, as I used to go out every night to pray, one of my wives used to ask me where I had been and I used to tell her, 'I have been outside'. I was afraid to pray in the hut, and one night I went out to pray again and she followed me and heard me pray aloud, but I did not know she had followed me. She asked me again where I had been when I returned, 'Where have you been?' 'Just outside.' She then said, 'I know where you have been; you went out to pray. Why do you not pray in the house? Why do you go out when you go to pray?'

"I felt very glad in my mind for her to say so, and was now greatly encouraged. After that I prayed in the house, and also before our meals, as we never used to pray before meals. But then again when visitors and strangers came to my house, I used to be afraid to pray. My wife then said, 'Why did you not pray when these people were here? You should not be afraid of anybody.' After that I used to pray even when strangers were present, morning and evening openly, and go out and pray secretly too.

"I was then anxious to read the Bible for myself and got someone to teach me the alphabet in my house. I have now managed by the Lord's help to read the First Zulu Reader, and have now begun the Second Zulu Reader. I want you to give me a Bible now as I can read a little, so that I can read it at worship. But I want you to pray for me, as I am a very great sinner. I feel my heart very bad."

65

Mr Radasi gave the new chief a Bible and found that he could read it fairly well. Some time later Sigogo told his minister that he was troubled by the European farmer, who asked him to work on Sabbath in the fields and to dip the cattle. Sigogo firmly refused to do this.

In a letter to Mr Cameron Mr Radasi wrote how pleased they were at Ingwenya to have received copies of the first 24 Psalms in si-Xhosa metre. Copies had already been sold to those who could read. Mr Radasi stressed that care was to be taken to read the line carefully in all the congregations so that people who could not read would also be able to join in the singing.

Mr Radasi was grateful for the suggestion of the home Church that the money collected for the Psalm books should be given to the poor. Mr Radasi wrote: "We have many destitute people and they have no means to buy clothes to go to church. It is specially difficult when they are ill and cannot pay for medicine. Most missionaries have boxes of medicines sent to them and they give them out to their people and sometimes to the people of other churches."

CHAPTER FIFTEEN

The People and Their School

MANY of those who attended the services at Ingwenya and elsewhere had several miles to walk over paths which were often crossed by ruts and ditches, caused by previous rainy seasons with their torrential rains. Many of the women were poorly clad, and almost every woman had a baby on her back, and often a small child in her arms. Heathen women, when they did appear occasionally at a funeral or a wedding, were bare-headed, unlike the church-going women who always wore a scarf or cap on their heads. The heathen women also had an ill-at-ease expression, which changed to a warm, friendly look when the Word of God was blessed to them.

Some women had unsympathetic husbands who expected their wives to work in the fields on the Lord's Day while they themselves went to a beer-drink. On the other hand the husband might be a converted man and have three or four wives. Such men were expected by the Church to keep the first wife as the true wife and to send the others back to their parents' homes.

By 1922 there would be about 100 children attending Ingwenya school. It can be seen that the attitude of the parents to the education of their children altered considerably. Boys usually came to school at an older age than the girls, perhaps at 10 or even 12 years of age. The reason for this was that the boys were required to herd the cattle, as the maize and other crops were grown in open fields with no fencing to protect them. When a younger brother became available to herd the cattle the older boy was free to attend school.

The children came to school in the morning having eaten nothing since the evening meal of the previous day. The first family meal was eaten about 11 am and, even if the mothers thought of cooking porridge for the children in the early morning, they probably could not afford it or they were already busy working in the fields from near daybreak.

It was difficult for mothers to provide clothing for the children, and they were scantily clad. This did not matter so much in the warm weather, but in the winter they often shivered with the cold.

The school buildings erected at out-stations did not last long, and had to be constantly repaired because of the ravages of the white ants, or termites, which attacked the wooden poles and, if there was nothing to stop them, would make their way to the thatch and destroy it very quickly. Books left on the earthen floor of the class-room over the weekend, would be in tatters when the pupils returned to school the following week, as a result of the termites' activity. Narrow openings in the classroom walls admitted some of the sunshine, but at times classes were held under a tree, and a blackboard tied to the branch of a tree could be seen swaying in the breeze!

But from these primitive schools came many children who had mastered the basic skills of reading, writing and arithmetic. And they had a head knowledge — slight, but correct — of Biblical truth. Some progressed from an outside school of a low standard to Ingwenya, and a few went for higher education elsewhere, and were a credit to their teachers and parents. Better still, a number were converted and were a blessing to their fellow-men.

Thatched classrooms at Zenka school.

In early summer, when the fields of maize were ready for harvesting, the little thatched school would present a charming picture surrounded, perhaps, by a few flowering trees, with fields of maize as a background.

CHAPTER SIXTEEN

Trials and Conversions

DURING the next year, 1916, the people at Ingwenya had to contend with a severe drought. Its effects were felt all the more because the sides of the well caved in. The well was too badly damaged to be repaired, so they had to dig a new one 70 feet deep. It is interesting to note that John Hlazo, former father-in-law of Mr Radasi and a good friend, paid almost half the cost.

Mr Radasi was anxiously waiting to hear whether the remaining Psalms in si-Xhosa metre had been printed. He wrote to Mr Cameron: "I am sorry to say that I have not heard anything about the printing of the remaining Psalms, whether they have begun printing them or not; we all regret the delay. When I went to Cape Colony last December I visited Lovedale to see what progress had been made, but Professor Henderson said that they still had another work they were printing, but as soon as they were finished printing that work they would begin to print the Psalms."

Mr Radasi also had to report that Florida Mine had closed down — it was not profitable. "However," he went on, "we still hold services at a kraal close by. The headman of the kraal is Sibindwana; he said to us, 'People on mines always come and go. You had better hold services at my kraal as we are always here.' One of the headman's daughters has been converted and his son also, and they are very regular at the means of grace."

Another cheerful item in Mr Radasi's letter was that they had opened another preaching station at Chief Mhlahlo's place. The chief was living on a farm, known as Gravesend, about five miles from Ingwenya. The farmer did not live there but visited it occasionally. Before this time he had opposed the idea of having a church on his farm. The chief lent a hut of his own to hold services in until they were able to build a large square hut to use as a church. Kiwa, a young brother of the chief, was being educated at Ingwenya and was living with Mr Radasi. He had recently been converted.

In spite of trials and difficulties Mr Radasi pressed on with the work, but not in his own strength. "Pray for us," he wrote to a friend, "that the Lord may give us strength to perform the duties faithfully to which he has called us. We need the guidance of the Holy Spirit in everything we do. What our blessed Lord says is only too true: 'Without Me ye can do nothing.'"

"Our main object in keeping a school," Mr Radasi continued, "is that the people may learn to read their Bibles. It is there that they can learn the doctrine of our ruin by the Fall, redemption by the blood of Christ, and regeneration by the Holy Ghost. These are doctrines absolutely necessary to be taught to the heathen for salvation. It is very, very sad to think that some of those who are sent to teach the heathen put these doctrines into the background. Pray for me that I may be faithful in declaring the whole counsel of God and look only to the grace and power of God for success in my labours." God heard these prayers, and in Mr Radasi's letters there are accounts of some remarkable conversions.

In one such letter, he first tells of the epidemic of malaria that was sweeping the country: "The whole country is suffering from fever and many people have died from it. We also have lost some people at Bembesi and Ingwenya and some are still very ill. Kiwa Mhlahlo too has been very ill for

Children guiding a blind woman on her way to speak to a missionary.

over a month and has had to go home to Gravesend Farm. Harriet Mzamo, daughter of Mr Patrick Mzamo, is also very sick, though not as bad as she was before. She is at present teaching at our school at Induba at Chief Mhlahlo's kraal, though she is often interrupted from her work of teaching through illness. So I am kept very busy visiting the sick.

"I may here mention a case that I was called to, of an old heathen Matabele woman, who was very seriously ill. Her son who came to call me said that he did not know whether I would still find her alive, and that she had expressed a desire to see me, and so I went. I found the old woman very ill. She was left in a hut by herself, and the hut (was) closed, and they used to go now and then to peep into the hut to see if she had expired, as they were expecting her to die any minute. I found that they had already dug her grave. The heathen usually dig the grave before the person dies if they think the person is so

72

seriously ill that he or she cannot recover, so that the person can be buried at once.

"I found that she was quite conscious and that she could still speak distinctly and understand what was said, although very weak and ill. She said, 'I have dreamt a dream which has greatly alarmed me. I dreamt that I was on a journey and got to a big river, and on the other side of the river was a very beautiful place. Someone from that place spoke to me and said, "You cannot come into this place; you are very, very filthy, and you need to be washed in order to get there. All those that are in that beautiful place have all been washed. The road that the Matabele are walking on is a filthy road; you must go back and wash." After the person was speaking to me, whom I could not see clearly, I heard many, many voices saying, "Yes, it is quite true, the road that the Matabeles are walking on is very filthy. You must go back and wash."

"'After I told my people my dream they went to fetch many buckets of water to wash (me), but I told them that the water they had brought me would not do, and that they had better send for a minister at once. I could see that they thought I was out of my mind, and that I did not know what I was saying, and their intention was to call a witch-doctor to see what was the matter with me. But I firmly refused, and told them that a witch-doctor would do no good to me, and insisted on them sending for a minister. That is why I sent my son to come and call you. I had heard about you from my daughters who occasionally attend your church, and I want you to pray for me.'

"I then prayed for her and read the Word of God slowly to her. She listened very attentively while I was reading, and then began to weep. I continued to visit her every now and then and she recovered within a fortnight. I am glad to say she has now been converted and is a regular attender of our church. She lives at Libeni and I also go there now and then, and hold a service at the kraal. She seemed to realize that she was a great sinner and not fit to go to 'that beautiful place', and that God was right in sending her away, and that her desire was that God should wash her and fit her for 'that beautiful place'."

The wife of an old Ndebele man who said he knew the old King Mzilikazi, Lobengula's father, had a somewhat similar experience. "I was a very careless, godless woman," she told Mr Radasi, "and hated going to church and the people who went there." One night she dreamt that someone told her all that she had done, and what a wicked woman she was, and asked her where she expected to go when she died, as she had never opened her mouth in prayer. "I felt," she said, "very miserable. I went to church, but I found no peace. I thought there was no peace for me. I continued in great unhappiness, but one day in church these words read from the Word of God gave me relief: 'This is a faithful saying, and worthy of all acceptation, that Christ Jesus came into the world to save sinners; of whom I am chief.' I thought: If Christ came to save even the chief of sinners, I am that, and there is hope for me too. And then I felt glad."

CHAPTER SEVENTEEN

The Power of the Word of God

AS we have seen, Mr Radasi was greatly interested in the spiritual welfare of the young people in his congregations. He got a steady supply of Bibles from the British and Foreign Bible Society, both in English and in the local languages. These he distributed to the young people as soon as they learned to read.

Shortly after Mr Radasi opened a school at Ingwenya he asked the Church in Scotland to send him Zulu Bibles so that he could give a Bible to each of his pupils as soon as they learned to read. The first order was given to an Inverness bookseller who was able to supply Bibles at what the Church considered a reasonable price. However, they discovered that they had to pay as much as £2.75 to send out Bibles which cost only £3 altogether to buy. Mr Cameron discussed the difficulty with the British and Foreign Bible Society and afterwards Bibles were sent at a much lower price from the Society's depot in Johannesburg, and delivered to Bembesi without any charge for carriage.

Mr Cameron commented in 1916: "From the fact that so many Bibles have been distributed for the last 11 years, a considerable number of the Matabele must have been taught to read the Bible, which is the chief aim of Mr Radasi in teaching them. This we consider a promising feature of the effect of Mr Radasi's labours in that part of Matabeleland where he has been working."

The Mission under Mr Radasi had indeed made progress. That year he gave details of the places of worship and schools: "Our preaching places are at Ingwenya, Bembesi, Koco, Florida Mine, Sibindwana's kraal, Gravesend, and at Selukwe on the farm where Chief Garner Sojini is staying. In all those places we have built square huts to hold services in, with the exception of Selukwe, where we hold services in one of Chief Garner Sojini's huts, as the owner of the farm does not wish a church built on his farm. Services are held every Sabbath by our men where we have built churches, but I also go out occasionally to preach at these out-stations. The places where we have schools are Ingwenya, Induba and at Sibindwana's kraal.

"The practice of giving Bibles to those who can read is still being continued, and I think it is a very good practice. It is good that they should be acquainted with the Word of God. I take the Bible lessons myself every day in the day-school for those who can read; and to the rest of the school that cannot read I give a Bible lesson, and all seem to be anxious to learn how to read so that they might receive the gift of a Bible."

Mr Radasi then went on to give an encouraging example of a boy who made good use of one of these Bibles: "I may mention the case of Mrs Ntuli's boy, aged 14 years, who died recently. Joseph Ntuli loved his Bible, and when he was ill and laid up (in bed) he put it under his pillow and would open it and read it every now and then. When he himself could no longer read, he used to ask his mother to read him several chapters every day. The day that he died, his mother was about to give him his medicine as usual. He said, 'Mother, do not trouble yourself by giving me more medicine, and also take this plaster off that you have put on me. The whole world cannot help me with all their medicines. Leave these medicines alone, Mother.'

Boys on their way to school.

"He then took out his Bible from his pillow and opened it at the tenth chapter of Job and asked his mother to read it to him. After his mother had done this, he called for the Bible again and opened it at the fourteenth chapter of John, and asked his mother to read that for him. He then said, 'Jesus Christ is near me, Mother. I am not afraid to die, for I am trusting in Christ alone for salvation. I am sure that when I cross the river of death He will go with me. I am not at all afraid to die, Mother.' He then called his father, David Ntuli, and spoke very seriously to him. What he said to him I was not told, only that David Ntuli wept while he was being warned."

• CHAPTER EIGHTEEN •

Clouds and Sunshine

IN March 1917 Mr Radasi was writing about Kiwa Mhlahlo, brother of Chief Mhlahlo at Induba, and a former pupil at Ingwenya. He had been sent for teacher-training to Lovedale, but he had to return home because of chest trouble. Mr Radasi said: "I am sorry to say that Kiwa Mhlahlo is not able to return to Lovedale; his chest trouble has not left him. He is sometimes better; then his trouble returns and he is laid up. I understand from his people that this chest trouble is an old trouble of his. I would suggest that another boy be appointed to go to Lovedale in his stead. We have a promising youth named Paul Hlazo, who is in the Fourth Standard who I think could go at the beginning of next year if the Synod is willing, and we are still spared to see it. Kiwa is still teaching at his home at Induba."

The First World War was still raging, and Mr Radasi went on to report that some of the men attached to his congregations had gone to the war in German East Africa (now Tanzania). Some were drivers of wagons, while others had joined the Matabele regiment which was formed some time before. The reason these men went to the war was that they had to provide for their families. The effects of the war in Europe were also felt in Southern Rhodesia as everything had gone up in price.

In addition, the crops had failed as the rain had been late, and many of the people were starving.

At a later date Mr Radasi wrote: "We hear every now and then from our men in East Africa. I am sorry to say that I have seen in the newspapers that some have been seriously wounded, others slightly. I have not noticed that any of our people have been killed. They wish us to remember them in our prayers. Some of them were a great help to me in preaching in our out-stations. May the Lord by His Spirit apply the Word to their hearts and consciences." At the end of 1918 the men returned. Those who had been wounded had recovered. "It was a great joy," Mr Radasi wrote, "to see that none of the men was missing. Their European officers spoke very highly of them."

Although Mr Radasi refers to so many of the young people being ill and dying at the early age of 14 and 15, he does not say what they were suffering from. The only conclusion one can come to is that most of them were suffering from malaria of a very virulent type.

At the same time as Joseph Ntuli passed away, Mr Radasi wrote of a young Ndebele girl who realized she was a sinner and became an anxious seeker. Her old father was perplexed by her seriousness and anxiety. "Before we eat," he said, "she asks me to wait and she puts her hand in front of her face and speaks to someone we do not see; and after that she says, 'You can eat now'. And every night before we go to bed she asks us to kneel down and then she speaks things we do not understand to the person we do not see. Early in the morning she asks us to kneel down and then she speaks with tears in her eyes to someone we do not see. We cannot understand her now. Before she attended church she used to be a happy girl and now she complains of a bad heart, and I do not understand what she means as she is a very good girl and has never given any trouble at all." Mr Radasi understood, however, although the old man could not; the Spirit of God was convincing her of her sin and misery and drawing her to seek for salvation.

Mrs Julia Radasi and grandchildren.

Another girl who died at the early age of 14 had made remarkable progress in school during her two years there. She qualified for her Bible in the first year, and she had learned by heart Psalms 1, 15, 23 and 24, as well as the fifth chapter of Matthew and the third chapter of John. She was ill for only a week. "I was hurriedly called to her death-bed just a day before she died," Mr Radasi wrote, "as she was very anxious to see me and wished me to read and pray. She desired that the 139th Psalm should be read to her. When I had gone she told her father and mother that she expected it would be her last night on earth and that she was going to see the Saviour, that they were to give her Bible to her little brother, that it was the only inheritance she could leave him, and that they must see to it that her brother was never absent from school. Then she called them all and shook hands with them. The above were her last words."

Mr Cameron spoke about her when he addressed the next meeting of the Synod of the Free Presbyterian Church: "Those things are most touching and they should make a lasting impression on the minds of our young people in Scotland. Are the young Matabele boys and girls to be at the right hand of Christ at the great Day of Judgement, and shall our young people at home, who enjoy much greater privileges and opportunities, be at the left hand? I appeal to our young people to betake themselves to their knees in secret, for the Lord has given many promises, such as, 'Those that seek Me early shall find Me'."

• CHAPTER NINETEEN •
Home Life
Around Ingwenya

MR RADASI does not refer to the difficulties he must often
have met in going to visit the sick or elderly people belonging
to his own congregation or while travelling to the outlying
stations. At times he went to catechise the children at their
homes. In the rainy season he could not use his cart and
donkeys to carry him across the rivers, so he would have to
wade through some feet of water — but when peals of thunder
and flashes of lightning announced an approaching storm, it
was wise to be on the homeward side of the river.

Sometimes, when a sudden storm broke out, bringing
torrential rain where the river had its source, it caused a wall
of water to flow downstream and catch the unwary traveller
unexpectedly and sweep him off his feet as he crossed the
river. However, a large boulder here or there might help him to
recover his balance.

The homes of the people consisted of kraals - a group of
round huts built of pole and daga (mud) and thatched with
grass. If the owner of the kraal was a polygamist (someone
who had more than one wife) then each wife had her own hut,
and the children also had their own hut. The kitchen had a fire

Homes in "a line" at Ingwenya.

in the middle of the floor and the smoke escaped through the roof or out at the door; but if the weather was good, they usually cooked the food out of doors.

The women provided the simple furnishings of the home in the form of grass mats woven by themselves. They were used when entertaining visitors or when resting with the children in the afternoons or as sleeping mats at night. The baskets in the home were also woven by the women and often had decorative designs made with different coloured grasses. The larger baskets would be used for holding grain or meal, and the smaller baskets for collecting vegetables or wild fruits as well as for various purposes in the home. In the kitchen were clay pots, often decorated with different coloured clays and used for cooking, or for holding water or milk. The women showed great interest and skill in designing and making all these articles.

The floor was earthen, smoothed over with cow-dung and beaten until it shone. This kept down the dust and insects. The kraal was surrounded by a thick fence of twisted thorn trunks and branches, which made an impenetrable hedge. A space was left open during the day for the use of the family but it was closed at dusk in the same way, with twisted thorn trees and branches.

The cattle kraal was usually erected in front of the home so that any wild animal or thief would be detected at once. When the home was in an isolated part of the country, it was not uncommon for one or two lions to roar at one end of the cattle kraal causing the terrified cattle to rush to the opposite end of the kraal, and to break down the hedge in their desire to escape. The lions would then steal round the side of the kraal and kill the cattle as they emerged from the broken-down hedge.

His cattle had a special place in the heart of the African man. They were his only source of wealth, his only means of paying for his bride (lobola) and for the education of his children. In addition, they treated the cattle kraal as sacred to the men. No woman was allowed to approach it, and lively debates were often held there by local headmen.

Discipline in the home was strict. Children were taught to respect and obey their parents and the older members of the family. Girls rarely left their homes except to go to school and were in the constant company of their mothers. They learned much about the care of the home, of work in the fields and of caring for the small children in the family. From a very early age the boys looked after the goats and sheep, and eventually they were entrusted with the care of the cattle. The oxen all had their own names, and their own places when yoked for work in the cart or wagon, as any mistake in placing them in the team caused trouble among the oxen. The boys became skilled in handling the oxen and other cattle. While herding the cattle the boys learned to recognise the various plants and shrubs, birds and insects, and the legends connected with them.

In the early days the only source of sugar was in the bee-hives hidden in hollow tree trunks. It required skill to avoid the infuriated bees when their hives were disturbed. In later years sugar-cane was brought from South Africa. There were many snakes, and in the rainy season they were a constant menace as they emerged from their holes. That was one reason why there were no evening church services at Ingwenya and the other places. A bite or sting from a cobra or a puff-adder could be very painful, if not fatal. A black mamba was known to pursue a boy on his bicycle when he accidentally went over its tail.

When Mr Radasi arrived at a kraal he would call out a greeting at the entrance to the hedge, "Ekuhle" (It is well). A voice would return the greeting from one of the huts and he would enter the enclosure to be greeted by the owner of the kraal and by the women, who would curtsey as they shook hands. Mr Radasi would then be invited to enter one of the huts, where he would be offered a chair or stool to sit on. The master of the house would also sit on a stool, but the mother and children would sit on grass mats spread on the earthen floor. In a Christian home the minister and any other visitors would be treated with the greatest courtesy.

After some opening remarks the minister would question the children on the Bible verses and stories they had learned in school, and on the Shorter Catechism, as he offered up a silent prayer that the parents also would benefit. He expected those children who could read to memorize the Shorter Catechism answers. He found it a good practice to go round the homes catechising the children; in this way the parents who might be heathen were hearing the Word of God explained. Mr Radasi, no doubt, would conclude his visit by reading a portion of Scripture, perhaps singing a few verses of a Psalm, and with prayer.

CHAPTER TWENTY

A Blessing Through Prayer

MR RADASI noticed that many pupils seemed to be very fond of their Bibles and that they continued to read them after they left school. One of the boys, whom we shall call Temba, received a Bible like everyone else when he learned to read. When he left school, Temba found work at a mine and was given a hut to live in. A heathen boy, who also came to the mine to work, was sent to live in the same hut. Temba said afterwards: "I used to read the Bible and pray every night and morning, and the heathen boy did not like it at all. He said, 'Why do you trouble me? You read what I do not understand, and you pray to One you cannot see. I do not like what you are doing. You are trying to teach me new customs. I came to seek work. We never pray at our home, and I hate this custom of yours, and if you continue this custom I shall leave the place altogether.'"

Temba did not yield. He said later: "I continued to read and pray every morning and night and he continued to show his dislike to what I was doing until one day, early in the morning while it was still dark, I heard him cry out, 'Get up and let us pray; I like praying now. I have tried it myself, everything seems to be new with me now. When I begin the day with prayer, I find my work light and easy, and I do it cheerfully.

Tell me more about God and His Christ. I like to hear about them now.' He now used to listen very attentively to the Word of God, and wanted to know more and more about Christ and his great salvation for sinners."

Temba also told about a stranger who had recently been employed at the mine and visited them in their hut one evening. After they had worship as usual, the stranger was silent for some time and seemed to be in deep thought. Then he broke out in these words: "I am glad to see that you are praying, boys. Keep on praying, my boys. There is a God in reality and He does hear prayers. I will now tell you of a true incident that happened to me. Before the railway line was made from Bulawayo to Salisbury (now Harare), goods used to be transported by ox-waggon. I was a driver for some traders on one of their ox-waggons going to Salisbury. They treated me very cruelly on the way, and so I decided to run away from them. I left them one day and escaped. I kept away from the main road and followed the footpath.

"I had not gone very far when I saw a lion in front (of me) coming towards me at a rapid pace. I turned back to where I came from. To my surprise I saw another lion coming towards me from that side. A lion in front of me, and a lion at the back of me, and both coming to me! It was a hopeless case. I looked round to see if there was a tree to climb; I could not see any; and both lions were coming nearer and nearer to me. I now lost all hope of escape. Just at that time I seemed to hear a voice saying, 'Pray!' I knelt down and prayed at once, and as soon as I got up I saw both lions running away from me as fast as they could, and so I was saved from them. Boys, keep on praying. There is a God in reality and He does answer prayers."

Mr Radasi also told of an old woman who had been one of the wives of King Lobengula: "She lived at Induba, and was a member in full communion with our church there. She was converted two years ago. When she became ill her friends took her away for a change to a place 20 miles from Induba. The change did her no good, and she became worse and worse, and they had to bring her home again after she had been there for six weeks. And when she returned she was so ill that she could not speak any more. I went to see her on Wednesday, just a day after she had returned, and read the Bible and prayed, but she had lost her power of speech and she passed away on Friday. They say that just about two hours before she died she said in a loud voice, 'I am leaning on Christ alone for salvation'. Those were the only words she was heard to speak since she returned home."

Mr Radasi knew that one minister among so many people was not enough. As he thought about it, he wrote, "I would be very glad if the Lord would raise up a young man here to go to Scotland to be trained for the ministry. I had in my mind Kiwa Mhlahlo, the boy we first sent to Lovedale, but his health so broke down that he had to return home before he had even finished a year, and so I was disappointed. The difficulty is this, that the majority of boys leave school after they have learned their own language only, si-Xhosa or Zulu. I cannot say (anything) yet about the lad we have sent to Lovedale. May the Lord Himself put into the mind of a truly converted lad a desire to be trained for the ministry!"

He spoke too about other things he needed, but these could be more easily supplied: "I am greatly in need of a cart and mule for visiting the out-stations, especially in the rainy season, as the bicycle is of no use in wet weather. I have an opportunity of visiting the out-stations whenever I can go, as there are always people ill with fever. A new cart would cost £30 and a mule £20 to £25. Mules are better than horses in this hot country."

What he saw of the saving power of the Holy Spirit encouraged Mr Radasi very much, but on the other hand there were trials of various kinds from time to time. With sadness he reported the death of one of his old elders, a man who had been a great support to him: "He was over 70 years of age, and greatly devoted to our Cause here. He was a greatly exercised Christian and very fond of his Bible. During his illness he had it under his pillow. He often used to complain of his sinfulness and he was assured that there was no salvation apart from the sovereign grace of God."

Mr Radasi also wrote at this time of a very old man in the congregation at Sibindwana's kraal at Florida Mine. This man used to say that as a young man he knew Mzilikazi well. He and his wife wanted to come to church, but they had no fence around their fields to keep the goats from destroying the crops. "We like to listen to the Word of God," the old man explained, "so this is what we do: I mind the goats one Sabbath and she goes to church. Then she minds the goats next Sabbath and I go to church." His wife said that the day he died he seemed to be fighting with enemies that no one could see. At last he cried to the enemies, "I do not belong to you any more; I belong to the Lord". Then the enemies went away. "I saw a happy smile on his face," said his wife, "and after that he never spoke again."

Mr Cameron saw the account of this man's last days as evidence that the Holy Spirit was still working powerfully among the people in Matabeleland, and he was deeply thankful that it was so. "It should arouse all our praying people," he reminded the Church in Scotland, "to wrestle with the Lord that He would make that great wilderness a Garden of Eden."

In 1918 a great epidemic of influenza swept through Europe; shortly afterwards it reached South Africa and then Matabeleland. Mr Radasi described how serious its effects were, for it was before the discovery of antibiotics: "Your letter arrived when my wife and family were all laid up with Spanish influenza. Nearly every family at Bembesi and in Bulawayo was affected. There have been very many deaths from it here. At Kimberley, South Africa, 4,400 Africans died from it, and 597 white people, and in King William's Town, South Africa, 7,000 Africans. In Rhodesia no accurate account has been kept of the death of Africans, but reports from all parts of the country speak of a very heavy death toll. The hand of the Lord has been heavy upon us because of our sins and forsaking of Him, but there seems to be no sign of true repentance. That is the sad part of it."

An outside lesson at Mbuma school.

Mr Radasi was anxious to secure young men and women of the Church who would teach in his schools. He wrote of one pupil whom he was anxious to send to Lovedale: "I have a young Ndebele girl whose father and mother are members of our Church. She has been in our school for many years and is now in Standard Five. She and her parents are very anxious that she would go to Lovedale to be trained as a teacher, (and then) to come and teach the girls here, but they have no means to send her to Lovedale. I think she would be very useful here if properly trained. She could go at the beginning of next year if our Church would support her. We have now over 100 children in our school here and the Inspector says there ought to be three teachers in this school now, one principal and two assistants. We would like teachers belonging to our Church to teach the children."

90

In 1920 Mr Cameron could report some further progress, for a few of Mr Radasi's pupils had gone on to further education: "There are three studying at Lovedale, two girls and a boy, at the expense of the Church. One of them went there quite recently. Mr Radasi sent me the certificates of those who were there for some time. They have been a credit to themselves and the Mission. There are others at Lovedale from Bembesi, but their parents pay for them." Obviously there was a response to Mr Radasi's appeal for funds to support a girl at Lovedale because Mr Cameron went on to thank the friends who sent contributions to help her.

CHAPTER TWENTY-ONE

Two Deputies from Scotland

IN 1920, with the First World War over at last, Mr Radasi was reminding the Synod of his earlier request that a minister from Scotland would visit the Mission: "We would very much like one of our ministers to visit our Church here this year, either at the end of August or September, or next year during the spring. I am sure all our people would be very glad, and they would highly appreciate the visit. It would be a great help to our Cause here."

You can imagine Mr Radasi's delight when he heard that Rev Neil Cameron and Mr Angus Fraser were to come as deputies from the Church in Scotland. After the usual sea voyage and the train journey from Cape Town, the deputies arrived in Bulawayo in March 1921. Mr Cameron wrote: "Shortly after our arrival Rev J B Radasi appeared. He gave us a very hearty welcome and expressed his joy and thankfulness at seeing us. I need not say that we were overjoyed at meeting him, especially because he looked so well."

Mr Radasi, Mr Cameron and Mr Fraser went on by train to Bembesi, a distance of 28 miles. There they were met by a large number of office-bearers and other men from the Mission.

Mr Cameron wrote: "A few can speak English fairly well, a good many can understand a little and can speak a few words, while many were like ourselves, understanding not one word, but the expression of joy on their faces revealed their inner feelings better than the most eloquent speeches could have done, and was far more convincing."

Their luggage was placed on a four-wheeled wagon drawn by eight strong bullocks. Mr Radasi's mule, Cape cart and driver carried the four men to Ingwenya. Mrs Radasi met them on their arrival and showed the same happy feelings on meeting them. On the following Friday about 30 men came, some of them having walked several miles, to welcome the deputies and to express their thankfulness to them for having come so far.

On the Sabbath morning about 200 people gathered, some of whom had come several miles to the church. They listened with rapt attention to Mr Cameron preaching and Mr Radasi interpreting. The beauty of the Psalm singing amazed Mr Cameron. The congregation sang in four parts correctly and with much feeling. Mr Cameron said later that their experience in Africa was the most enjoyable they ever had because of how clearly he and Mr Fraser saw the fruit of the gospel among the people.

The next Sabbath the sacrament of the Lord's Supper was observed, in the open air. About 300 people were present at the first service, and 64 of them sat at the Lord's Table. Several young men who were employed in Bulawayo travelled to Ingwenya on the Saturday for the communion services and returned to Bulawayo on the Monday morning. Mr Cameron said afterwards: "As regards seriousness and good order all behaved exceedingly well. I could not but remember the Scripture, 'The wilderness and the solitary place shall be glad for them, and the desert shall rejoice and blossom as the rose'."

On the Monday, the final day of the communion services, heavy rain continued to fall at intervals and this prevented many of those living at a distance from being present at the services. As Mr Cameron wrote: "Travelling through the bush and through grass sometimes over six feet high, with rain pouring in torrents, required determination on the part of the congregation to hear the gospel. About 80 men and women were present."

During the first week of April one of the school inspectors in Bulawayo arrived in a wagon pulled by eight mules. Mr Cameron described their first visit: "After Mr Lenfesty's arrival, we decided that we would examine two of the side-schools on the following day. We left Ingwenya about 7 am for the school at Induba. There were 14 boys and 30 girls on the roll of this school. The children had very few books, no slates or blackboard or chalk or register. The inspector promised that he would order registers to be sent, and the Rev J B Radasi suggested that as he had procured a new blackboard for the school at Ingwenya the old one would be sent to Induba. . . . I asked Mr Radasi to provide, at the expense of the Church at home, books for the children whose parents were unable to pay for them and also for the children of such of the heathen who might refuse to provide their children with books; also that slates should be provided where it was found necessary and that chalk should be sent there. A large number of the children were not able to read the alphabet as they had not been long in school. A few could read their Bible in their own language tolerably well. After this school was examined, we came back to the wagon. Mr Lenfesty had ordered his driver to have breakfast ready for us in the open veldt, beside the wagon, at 10 am."

The party then set off for Morven, ten miles away, over a rough path through tall, tawny-coloured grass until they reached Morven. There they found a school built, like the one at Induba, of pole and daga (mud) with a thatched roof. There were 11 boys and 19 girls on the roll. Here too several of the young children had not been very long in the school, but there were others who read the Bible very well. They were questioned about the parables and answered very well. From Morven the party moved on to the main school at Ingwenya, where there were 56 boys and 48 girls on the register. The

Standard Four pupils showed a good knowledge of Arithmetic, they could read their own language fluently, and some of them had a good knowledge of English.

The school classes at Ingwenya, Induba and Morven for younger children were held only from 9 am to 11 am to allow the boys to go home to herd the cattle as there were no fences around their fields. The other classes were held from 10 am until 1 pm. Mr Cameron was impressed with the skilled way in which Mr Lenfesty had conducted the inspection, particularly in Bible knowledge. He also appreciated the kindness and consideration shown to Mr Radasi by the Director of Education in Salisbury. At this time Mr Radasi was doing all the teaching at Ingwenya.

Mr Cameron wrote to Scotland: "We have now visited three places where services are held every Sabbath by our elders: Bembesi, Induba and Morven, Mr Radasi going to each of them a Sabbath each quarter of the year. Mr Radasi also goes occasionally to preach in the kraals of the heathen bordering our Mission, and now and again one and another begins to attend the Sabbath services at Ingwenya." Mr Radasi very much appreciated the help he received from the elders who preached regularly in the out-lying churches.

On their third Sabbath at Ingwenya, Mr Cameron preached at Induba, where about 100 were present including Chief Bitisani, a local chief, and his three wives. The chief did not pretend to have embraced Christianity but he was kind to Mr Radasi and gave the deputies a friendly welcome. On their fourth Sabbath the deputies from Scotland went to Bembesi, about ten miles from Ingwenya, where there was a good brick church. A congregation of about 60 Fingoes gathered and listened most attentively. The school at Bembesi was later named Cameron School in honour of Rev Neil Cameron.

The deputies left for Scotland feeling that their experience exceeded all their expectations. Later, in addressing the Synod, Mr Cameron said, "The spiritual and numerical success of the Mission is beyond anything we expected". Mr Cameron also referred to the great kindness of the people: "They, out of their

John Mpofu.   Alexander Mpofu.

poverty, poured into Mr Radasi's house fowls, eggs, butter and sheep in such abundance that there was enough and to spare. We commend them to God and to the Word of His grace which is able to give them an inheritance among all them who are sanctified."

It is of interest that Chief Bitisani was in 1923 moved, with his people, by Government order, from the Ntabazinduna Reserve to the Shangani Reserve, now known as Nkayi, about 80 miles north-west of Ingwenya. (Ingwenya Mission was situated on the edge of Ntabazinduna Reserve.) The reason given for the order was that the Ntabazinduna reserve was over-stocked with cattle, every African family having the ambition to have as many cattle as possible; cattle were their only source of money. Parents sold their cattle to pay school fees or to pay the bride price, known as lobola, when their son married.

96

Chief Bitisani set off for Shangani, but it was with great reluctance that many of his people followed him. At that time Shangani was thickly forested, and many wild animals roamed there, including lion, leopard, elephant and wild dogs. The rivers were alive with crocodiles, and there were many cases of malaria. After settling in Shangani the chief sent a request to Mr Radasi for a preacher and a teacher for his people. The London Missionary Society had already begun work in one part of the Reserve, but Chief Bitisani insisted that he wished to have a Free Presbyterian preacher.

In 1923 John Mpofu, an elder in Mr Radasi's congregation at Ingwenya, offered to go to Shangani, taking with him as a teacher his son, Alexander, a fine young Christian. They had many troubles in their new home, suffering persecution from the African people who were already living there. However, they persevered, and Alexander could write later to Rev John Tallach, Mr Radasi's successor as missionary at Ingwenya: "Not for all the money in the world would I have missed seeing the change which has come over the people here through the gospel and the school. More than that, I have a good hope of meeting in heaven some of my pupils who were blessed by my Bible teaching in school." It was in this providential way that the Free Presbyterian Church extended work to Nkayi, and later on to Zenka and Mbuma, also in the Shangani Reserve.

• CHAPTER TWENTY-TWO •
Help in Times of Trial

MR RADASI was going on with his work as faithfully as ever, and God was still giving His blessing. Mr Radasi tells of visiting Induba, where a young girl was dying: "I found her very ill, but still conscious. She said she was very glad to see me and that her parents, who are heathen, were not willing that I should be called, but she insisted. She desired me to read the fourteenth chapter of John's Gospel. She told me that she had been very much troubled by her sins, and that these words had given her relief and comforted her: 'Let not your heart be troubled; ye believe in God, believe also in Me. In my Father's house are many mansions; if it were not so, I would have told you. I go to prepare a place for you.' She also warned her heathen parents to seek Christ now, otherwise they would never go to those mansions above, where she was going. Then again she spoke about the Sabbath, what a delight it was to her as the day on which she heard the Word of God. This girl had been converted for over a year and had never missed a service."

As soon as the rain came, mosquitoes became a plague, carrying the germs of malaria. Mr Radasi told Mr Cameron: "There seem to be a lot of mosquitoes of the larger size this year; the long green grass is full of them. They enter into

Paul Magaya Ncube and Philemon Ndebele, church elders in Zenka.

houses and so many people are suffering from fever in the whole district. Kiwa Mhlahlo's mother at Induba died of it and also another woman at Ingwenya. Both of them were members of our Church. Mrs Ntuli, one of the women who looked after you when you were here is also dangerously ill, and several others are laid up. Kiwa Mhlahlo did not follow Chief Bitisani (to the Shangani reserve). He is still as regular as ever in attending the services."

In 1922 there was a great drought, and the crops sown in November and December were a failure. There was no grass for the cattle and water was becoming very scarce. Famine set in and great numbers of people were on the point of starvation. Mr Radasi wrote: "The Government has begun to send relief, one bag of maize per family for seed. We are very grateful for the money from Scotland to supplement the Government aid." (He was referring to the fact that the Church's Synod had been told how bad things were and decided to send assistance.)

Some of the European farmers allowed the people to graze cattle on their farms. One farmer gave widows a regular supply of mealie-meal (maize). Nevertheless, the African people suffered greatly and lost many cattle. There was early rain in October of that year and Mr Radasi assured Mr Cameron that there would be an early crop of maize, but Mr Cameron insisted that the people should be supplied with maize until the new crop was ripe.

By 1922 the pupils in five schools numbered 301, a remarkable number at a time when very few children attended school. The schools were at Ingwenya, Bembesi, Manxeleni, Induba and Sibindwana's kraal. There were three students at Lovedale, sent there and paid for by the Church, and all doing well. Some parents had sent their children to Mashonaland for industrial training and others sent their children to Tiger Kloof, a teacher-training centre in Bechuanaland (now Botswana). It was much cheaper to send pupils to Tiger Kloof as it was just across the border in Botswana, whereas Lovedale was 1,000 miles away.

At this time 500 copies of the whole Psalter in si-Xhosa arrived from Lovedale, to the great joy of Mr Radasi and his people. He had waited for this over many years. The first consignment of 1,000 copies of the first 24 Psalms had been received in 1914. The delay in producing the complete Psalter was largely due to the fact that paper was very scarce during the First World War. It is interesting to learn that the Psalter was also much appreciated by the Presbyterian Church of South Africa. A South African religious magazine reviewed the first part of the book while the First World War was still going on and said, "What a treasure we have in the si-Xhosa Psalter for these days of sorrow and desolation".

In the 1922 Free Presbyterian Synod, Mr Cameron referred to a letter from the Synod of Kafraria, South Africa, expressing their friendship and their appreciation for the work accomplished by the Free Presbyterian Church in printing the Psalms in si-Xhosa metre. The Free Presbyterian Synod suggested that the Synod of Kafraria use their valuable influence in persuading the African churches to use this Psalm book as their only praise-book in public worship.

In August 1923 Mr Radasi wrote to Mr Cameron to tell him that he was suffering from diabetes and was no longer able to visit the out-stations, but was going on with his work at Ingwenya. Mr Cameron got in touch with the Superintendent of the Western Infirmary in Glasgow, who advised him to send Mr Radasi to Johannesburg, South Africa. Mr Cameron wrote to the Superintendent of the main hospital in Johannesburg, and assured him that all expenses would be paid if they accepted Mr Radasi as a patient. Mr Radasi, with one of his deacons, set off for Johannesburg at the beginning of November 1923, and returned to the Mission at the end of December in much better health. He was put on a strict diet, which proved helpful. Mr Radasi very much appreciated the kind treatment and consideration he received in the Johannesburg hospital.

The state of Mr Radasi's health made it all the more necessary that there should be another minister to help him.

Back in 1916 Mr Cameron had told members of Synod: "I desire to notice here a subject that has already been before the Synod repeatedly, that the Lord would raise up a young man in the Church at home to go to Africa to carry on the work of the Mission there with our worthy friend and brother, Mr J B Radasi. It would also be very desirable that all the praying people in our Church should remember at the throne of grace the necessity of this being done, for we are asked to pray the Lord of the harvest to send forth labourers to His own harvest. We have full confidence that, if this were done, the Lord would provide someone moved by the Spirit to proceed to South Africa."

In the end these prayers were answered when a young man offered himself for service in the Mission in Africa. He was John Tallach, the son of fine Christian parents; his father, Andrew Tallach, was a Church missionary in the Island of Raasay. John Tallach had served with the armed forces on the battlefields of Europe in the First World War (1914-18) and when he returned from France in 1918 he prepared for the ministry by taking the usual course in arts and divinity. He also took a course in tropical medicine in London and a short course in dentistry. It was said of Mr Tallach many years later: "He possessed many fine qualities of mind and heart, a strong physique, and an extraordinary measure of patience and practical shrewdness, which, consecrated by divine grace, made him a most successful missionary."

Mr Radasi was very pleased when he heard that Mr Tallach intended to join him in the work at Ingwenya. "His presence with me here," he wrote, "will be a great help to me and to our people. It is hoped that the Lord will spare him and give him grace and strength, and make him, by the Holy Spirit, a vessel fit for the Master's use. The harvest is great; the labourers are few. We need to pray the Lord of the harvest to send forth labourers into His vineyard who will faithfully preach the riches of Christ, and tell sinners their great need of repentance toward God and reconciliation through faith in the atonement made by our Lord Jesus Christ."

Mrs Julia Radasi in a Scotch cart.

In a letter written in March 1924 Mr Radasi said he was in much better health since he had returned from Johannesburg, and he thanked Mr Cameron for making arrangements to send him there. Mr Radasi described the difficulty they had in building a new school-room at Ingwenya. He was thankful that the school itself had been erected in 1923 when there was plenty thatching grass and water. The droughts of other years might have made it impossible.

At a communion in Ingwenya on Sabbath March 23, the church was so crowded that some of the people had to remain outside. "I only wished that Mr Tallach had been with us, too. Trials and difficulties there are in plenty, but hitherto hath the Lord helped us."

Then at the beginning of September Mr Radasi sent a letter to say that symptoms of his diabetes had reappeared in July. This attack was much less severe than before and he was able to attend to all his duties, but he did feel weaker. Then, after his doctor prescribed some medicine, he felt much better. Mr Cameron wrote to him asking him to contact the Johannesburg hospital if he felt that it would be more helpful to get treatment there. Mr Cameron acknowledged that he felt real anxiety about what would happen on the Mission if it would be the Lord's will to remove Mr Radasi.

This anxiety made Mr Cameron and others realise that no time should be lost in having Mr Tallach ordained so that he might reach Africa as soon as possible. They told Mr Tallach about the situation and, although he did not intend to sail until January, he placed himself unreservedly at the disposal of the Church. Steps were taken at once to have him ordained and to secure his passage to Cape Town. He was ordained on September 12 and he sailed from Liverpool on October 11. Before he left, Dr Johnston, a member of the Free Presbyterian Church in Glasgow, gave him some medical instruments and a quantity of insulin. Dr Johnston was thinking of Mr Radasi's diabetes when he gave Mr Tallach the insulin and he showed him how to administer it.

Mr Radasi was told that Mr Tallach's ship was due to arrive in Cape Town on October 31, and that he could expect him at Bembesi on November 6 by the mail train. In reply he expressed the great joy with which the good news of Mr Tallach's arrival was received by himself, his office-bearers and all the people of the Mission. After the people knew when to expect Mr Tallach to arrive they began at their own expense to build two new huts and a kitchen for his use.

CHAPTER TWENTY-THREE

Taken Home

MR RADASI was expected to introduce the young missionary to the people and to the everyday running of the Mission, to advise and instruct him about the character and customs of the people, and to help him in learning the language. As events proved, and as sometimes happens, this was not God's purpose.

On 4 November 1924 Mr Radasi went the ten miles from Ingwenya Mission to Bembesi Siding (trains stopped there, but there were no platforms) to board the train for Bulawayo where he was to meet the Rev John Tallach, who was due to arrive on November 6. At Bembesi Siding Mr Radasi crossed in front of a stationary train to board the train coming in on the other side. As he was walking between the stationary train and the next set of rails, the incoming train swept in fast and Mr Radasi was pulled beneath the wheels and killed instantly.

So two days later it was a police officer and a deacon from Ingwenya — not Mr Radasi — who met Mr Tallach in Bulawayo. One can imagine his distress on hearing the very sad news of Mr Radasi's death. He went on at once by goods train to Bembesi and arrived in time for the funeral, which was attended by all the people of the district, black and white.

Mr Radasi's grave.

Mr Tallach addressed the large gathering from the words in John 14:3, "And if I go and prepare a place for you, I will come again, and receive you unto myself; that where I am, there ye may be also". Mr Tallach wrote later: "The whole proceedings in connection with the funeral were not only orderly but such as one would desire. The whole service bespoke their love for their pastor and his influence over them. It was evident that the sorrow of Mr Radasi's people was mingled with an intelligent joy in the belief that all was well with their pastor."

The people throughout the Church in Scotland were deeply shocked and saddened at the news. They felt great sympathy for Mrs Radasi and the children in their sore bereavement, and for Mr Tallach in losing his fellow-minister — whose guidance and help would have been so valuable — and for the people who had lost a spiritual father and a devoted pastor.

The fact that Mr Tallach arrived after Mr Radasi's death, and that he knew so little about the running of the Mission placed him in a very difficult position, especially when he did not know the language spoken by the people. However, because Mr Cameron had been to the Mission he was able to give Mr Tallach much useful advice. It was only God who could see into the future, and Mr Cameron acknowledged that it was the Lord who had sent him to the Mission in 1921, as it enabled him to learn on the spot everything about the working of the Mission and to pass the information on to Mr Tallach.

Tributes poured in from government offices in Salisbury, and from all quarters of the country. The Director of Education in Salisbury wrote: "Although it is now a good many years since I last saw Mr Radasi, I have always followed his work with much interest, and have known him to be steadfast, loyal and devoted, without any trace of arrogance though living in surroundings which might easily have made even an upright and God-fearing man somewhat arrogant. . . . I know that his example was a pure one and am persuaded that his influence will remain among the people whom he served so long and so faithfully."

Rev John Tallach.

Shortly after arriving, Mr Tallach wrote: "While under the circumstances of such deep, widespread grief one might expect a certain amount of uncontrollable emotion to be seen, yet the spirit of the people was rather that of calm solemnity. I think it would be hard to find a more disciplined people under the circumstances. Some of the white people showed their sympathy, by way of kindness towards Mrs Radasi, while (some of the) heathen walked a considerable distance to express their sorrow.

"What the loss is to myself I cannot tell. I am as a man in a dream as yet. The schools were closed since Tuesday. After the funeral service I called the office-bearers and teachers to meet me, and I explained to them that, although Mr Radasi was removed, all the work of the mission would be carried on as heretofore. . . . It was natural that to their sorrow there was added a very real discouragement. His personal relations with them all were the means to a great extent of keeping their interest in the Mission alive, and when he was taken away they felt there was nothing to work for. They were told that, although the Lord takes away His servants when and how he pleases, yet He remains Himself with His Word, His gospel and His work, giving the assurance to those who undertake the labour for Him that He will bless them in their labour. They were also told that the sympathy of the whole Church in Scotland was going out to them, and that its purpose to go on and its interest remained. I am thankful to say that the Most High has given another spirit to them. One said, 'We must be strong in the work of the Lord'; and some are voicing the desire that the Lord would raise up a young man among them who might go to Scotland to be educated for the ministry and come back to be among them. May the Lord hear such a desire and answer it in His own time!

"On Sabbath we had the usual three services, with the children's meeting afterwards. Stephen Hlazo interprets for me, and the people say they understand quite well. One of the addresses was from Revelation 14:13, 'And I heard a voice from heaven saying into me, Blessed are the dead which die in the Lord from henceforth: Yea, saith the Spirit, that they may rest from their labours; and their works do follow them'. Mr Radasi, a week last Sabbath, asked the people of all the out-stations to come to Ingwenya. This they did and the church was filled with an attentive congregation."

"We should be thankful to the Lord," Mr Cameron said as he reported the news to the Synod, "that He so arranged it in His providence that Mr Tallach arrived in time to carry on the work without a break and also for the tact and wisdom with which Mr Tallach met the painful circumstances which confronted him on his arrival. We think that the Lord's guiding hand can be traced in the past in connection with our Mission in Matabeleland, and that the Synod should give all the glory to the Lord for all the goodness and mercy with which He followed our efforts to spread the knowledge of His name."

Mr Cameron went on to give the following tribute: "Mr Radasi was truly an eminently godly man. He served with the utmost faithfulness the Free Presbyterian Church of Scotland during 19 years. The Lord set many seals to his ministry and, we have no doubt, received him with the words, 'Well done, thou good and faithful servant, thou hast been faithful over a few things, I will make thee ruler over many things. Enter thou into the joy of thy Lord.' . . . He was endowed beyond many with wisdom, humility, self-denial and trustworthiness. His faith in the absolute inerrancy and infallibility of the Bible, together with entire dependence on the Holy Spirit as to the success of the Word preached . . . was the secret of his success. But the Lord in His inscrutable providence removed him from the field by a sudden death. The change to him was, we can have no doubt, everlasting happiness, and our duty is, 'Be still and know that I am God'."

So a faithful servant of the Lord Jesus Christ went to be with the Saviour. We believe it is true of his experience: "In Thy presence is fulness of joy; at Thy right hand there are pleasures for evermore."

CHAPTER TWENTY-FOUR

The Work Goes On

AFTER John Mpofu and his son Alexander moved to the Shangani Reserve in the year before Mr Radasi died, they built a church in which services were held on the Lord's Day and in which the children were taught during the week. The people of Morven, ten miles from Ingwenya, had been warned too that they would be moved from the farm on which they were living to one of the reserves, the nearest being Shangani. The Committee in Scotland advised that, if at all possible, they should move to the same area as Chief Bitisani had gone to, so that the missionary and school would be there ahead of them.

It is interesting to recall that there were three men living at Morven who later became elders in the Nkayi district and preached on behalf of the Free Presbyterian Church. Samuel Sithole settled with his family at Donsa Dam and was a much respected elder. Philemon Ndebele, father of the Rev A B Ndebele, settled at Zenka and was highly esteemed. Sandlana Mkandhla, who died at the age of 90, was a man powerful in prayer, and he made his home at Kataza, near Zenka.

Another Chief, who lived at Inyathi, about 25 miles north of Bembesi, sent men to Mr Tallach asking the Church to set up a Mission among them. "It seems that Ethiopia is stretching out

Waiting at the out-patients department of the Mbuma Hospital.

her hands to God," was Mr Cameron's comment on hearing of yet another request for a preacher and school.

If we turn to look at mission work in Zimbabwe today under the Free Presbyterian Church of Scotland we can see that it has increased greatly since the days of Rev J B Radasi, Rev John Tallach, and Rev Dr Roderick MacDonald, who came to the Mission only five years after Rev John Tallach. Many gracious men and women have gone to their eternal rest from the various congregations of the Church, but much remains to be done. For some years there were five African ministers, but two fine ministers, Rev B B Dube at Zenka and Rev A Mpofu in Bulawayo passed away at an early age, which was a great loss to the Church.

At Mbuma, in the Nkayi District, Rev Petros Mzamo has nine places of worship to supply with preachers each Lord's Day. He is ably supported by his elders. There is a 60-bedded

The church and John Tallach Secondary School at Ingwenya in the 1990s.

hospital at Mbuma with a doctor and trained staff. The hospital serves a population of 13,000, but owing to the lack of transport in some districts, and intervening rivers and other hazards, many people cannot make use of the services available at the hospital.

At Ingwenya, the scene of the first missionaries' work, Rev A B Ndebele has a large congregation, which is increased by around 600 boarding pupils who attend the John Tallach Secondary School. Rev A B Ndebele is also responsible for pulpit supply for four out-stations, for two churches in Bulawayo and for the spiritual care of Thembiso Children's Home, also in Bulawayo. He also has the willing and able help of elders.

Mr Radasi had hoped to begin mission work in Mashonaland, but two chiefs made it impossible because they were afraid they would not be able to keep their many wives and would also have to give up other heathenish practices. Now Rev Z Mazvabo, himself a Shona, has eight congregations in that part of the country — in the area of Zvishavane (Shabani).

The fields are white unto harvest. The great need is for the presence and blessing of the Holy Spirit, and for the earnest prayer of His people that He would send out labourers unto His harvest.